MCA 06

ANN LANDERS AND ABIGAIL VAN BUREN

ANN LANDERS AND ABIGAIL VAN BUREN

Virginia Aronson

CHELSEA HOUSE PUBLISHERS
PHILADELPHIA

Cover Photos: Globe Photos/ John Barrett (Ann Landers)
Globe Photos/ Michael Ferguson (Abigail Van Buren)

Chelsea House Publishers
EDITOR IN CHIEF Stephen Reginald
PRODUCTION MANAGER Pamela Loos
ART DIRECTOR Sara Davis
DIRECTOR OF PHOTOGRAPHY Judy L. Hasday
MANAGING EDITOR James D. Gallagher
SENIOR PRODUCTION EDITOR LeeAnne Gelletly

Staff for **Ann Landers and Abigail Van Buren**
SENIOR EDITOR Therese De Angelis
ASSISTANT EDITOR Rob Quinn
ASSOCIATE ART DIRECTOR Takeshi Takahashi
DESIGNER Keith Trego
PICTURE RESEARCHER Sandy Jones
COVER DESIGNER Emiliano Begnardi

The Chelsea House World Wide Web address is:
http://www.chelseahouse.com

First Printing
1 3 5 7 9 8 6 4 2

Library of Congress Cataloging-in-Publication Data

Aronson, Virginia.
Ann Landers and Abigail Van Buren / Virginia Aronson.
 p. cm.— (Women of achievement series)
Includes bibliographical references and index.
Summary: A biography of the twin sisters known for the advice they give in
their columns, "Ann Landers" and "Dear Abby."

ISBN 0-7910-5297-4—ISBN 0-7910-5298-2 (pbk.)

1. Landers, Ann—Juvenile literature. 2. Van Buren, Abigail, 1918—Juvenile literature.
3. Advice columnists—United States—Biography—Juvenile literature. 4. Women journalists—
United States—Biography—Juvenile literature. 5. Sisters—United States—Biography—Juvenile
literature. 6. Twins—United States—Biography—Juvenile literature. [1. Landers, Ann. 2. Van Buren,
Abigail, 1918- 3. Advice columnist. 4. Women—Biography.] I. Title. II. Women of achievement.
PN4874.L23 A76 1999
070'.92'273—dc21
[B]   99-050097

NOTE: Abigail Van Buren uses the registered trademark "Dear Abby"® as the title of her column.

CONTENTS

WOMEN of ACHIEVEMENT

Jane Addams
SOCIAL WORKER

Madeleine Albright
STATESWOMAN

Marian Anderson
SINGER

Susan B. Anthony
WOMAN SUFFRAGIST

Clara Barton
AMERICAN RED CROSS FOUNDER

Margaret Bourke-White
PHOTOGRAPHER

Rachel Carson
BIOLOGIST AND AUTHOR

Cher
SINGER AND ACTRESS

Hillary Rodham Clinton
FIRST LADY AND ATTORNEY

Katie Couric
JOURNALIST

Diana, Princess of Wales
HUMANITARIAN

Emily Dickinson
POET

Elizabeth Dole
POLITICIAN

Amelia Earhart
AVIATOR

Gloria Estefan
SINGER

Jodie Foster
ACTRESS AND DIRECTOR

Betty Friedan
FEMINIST

Althea Gibson
TENNIS CHAMPION

Ruth Bader Ginsburg
SUPREME COURT JUSTICE

Helen Hayes
ACTRESS

Katharine Hepburn
ACTRESS

Mahalia Jackson
GOSPEL SINGER

Helen Keller
HUMANITARIAN

**Ann Landers/
Abigail Van Buren**
COLUMNISTS

Barbara McClintock
BIOLOGIST

Margaret Mead
ANTHROPOLOGIST

Edna St. Vincent Millay
POET

Julia Morgan
ARCHITECT

Toni Morrison
AUTHOR

Grandma Moses
PAINTER

Lucretia Mott
WOMAN SUFFRAGIST

Sandra Day O'Connor
SUPREME COURT JUSTICE

Rosie O'Donnell
ENTERTAINER AND COMEDIAN

Georgia O'Keeffe
PAINTER

Eleanor Roosevelt
DIPLOMAT AND HUMANITARIAN

Wilma Rudolph
CHAMPION ATHLETE

Elizabeth Cady Stanton
WOMAN SUFFRAGIST

Harriet Beecher Stowe
AUTHOR AND ABOLITIONIST

Barbra Streisand
ENTERTAINER

Elizabeth Taylor
ACTRESS AND ACTIVIST

Mother Teresa
HUMANITARIAN AND
RELIGIOUS LEADER

Barbara Walters
JOURNALIST

Edith Wharton
AUTHOR

Phillis Wheatley
POET

Oprah Winfrey
ENTERTAINER

Babe Didrikson Zaharias
CHAMPION ATHLETE

"REMEMBER THE LADIES"

MATINA S. HORNER

"Remember the Ladies." That is what Abigail Adams wrote to her husband John, then a delegate to the Continental Congress, as the Founding Fathers met in Philadelphia to form a new nation in March of 1776. "Be more generous and favorable to them than your ancestors. Do not put such unlimited power in the hands of the Husbands. If particular care and attention is not paid to the Ladies," Abigail Adams warned, "we are determined to foment a Rebellion, and will not hold ourselves bound by any Laws in which we have no voice, or Representation."

The words of Abigail Adams, one of the earliest American advocates of women's rights, were prophetic. Because when we have not "remembered the ladies," they have, by their words and deeds, reminded us so forcefully of the omission that we cannot fail to remember them. For the history of American women is as interesting and varied as the history of our nation as a whole. American women have played an integral part in founding, settling, and building our country. Some we remember as remarkable women who—against great odds—achieved distinction in the public arena: Anne Hutchinson, who in the 17th century became a charismatic religious leader; Phillis Wheatley, an 18th-century black slave who became a poet; Susan B. Anthony, whose name is synonymous with the 19th-century women's rights movement, and who led the struggle to enfranchise women; and in the 20th century, Amelia Earhart, the first woman to cross the Atlantic Ocean by air.

These extraordinary women certainly merit our admiration, but other women, "common women," many of them all but forgotten, should also be recognized for their contributions to American thought and culture. Women have been community builders; they have founded schools and formed voluntary associations to help those in need; they have assumed the major responsibility for rearing children, passing on from one generation to the next the values that keep a culture alive. These and innumerable other contributions, once ignored, are now being recognized by scholars, students, and the public. It is exciting and gratifying that a part of our history that was hardly acknowledged a few generations ago is now being studied and brought to light.

In recent decades, the field of women's history has grown from obscurity to a politically controversial splinter movement to academic respectability, in many cases mainstreamed into such traditional disciplines as history, economics, and psychology. Scholars of women, both female and male, have organized research centers at such prestigious institutions as Wellesley College, Stanford University, and the University of California. Other notable centers for women's studies are the Center for the American Woman and Politics at the Eagleton Institute of Politics at Rutgers University; the Henry A. Murray Research Center for the Study of Lives, at Radcliffe College; and the Women's Research and Education Institute, the research arm of the Congressional Caucus on Women's Issues. Other scholars and public figures have established archives and libraries, such as the Schlesinger Library on the History of Women in America, at Radcliffe College, and the Sophia Smith Collection, at Smith College, to collect and preserve the written and tangible legacies of women.

From the initial donation of the Women's Rights Collection in 1943, the Schlesinger Library grew to encompass vast collections documenting the manifold accomplishments of American women. Simultaneously, the women's movement in general and the academic discipline of women's studies in particular also began with a narrow definition and gradually expanded their mandate. Early causes, such as woman suffrage and social reform, abolition, and organized labor were joined by newer concerns, such as the history of women in business and the professions and in politics and government; the study of the family; and social issues such as health policy and education.

Women, as historian Arthur M. Schlesinger, jr., once pointed out, "have constituted the most spectacular casualty of traditional history. They have made up at least half the human race, but you could never tell that by looking at the books historians write." The new breed of historians is remedying that omission. They have written books about immigrant women and about working-class women who struggled for survival in cities and about black women who met the challenges of life in rural areas. They are telling the stories of women who, despite the barriers of tradition and economics, became lawyers and doctors and public figures.

The women's studies movement has also led scholars to question traditional interpretations of their respective disciplines. For example, the study of war has traditionally been an exercise in military and political analysis, an examination of strategies planned and executed by men. But scholars of women's history have pointed out that wars have also been periods of tremendous change and even opportunity for women, because the very absence of men on the home front enabled them to expand their educational, economic, and professional activities and to assume leadership in their homes.

The early scholars of women's history showed a unique brand of courage in choosing to investigate new subjects and take new approaches to old ones. Often, like their subjects, they endured criticism and even ostracism by their academic colleagues. But their efforts have unquestionably been worthwhile, because with the publication of each new study and book another piece of the historical patchwork is sewn into place, revealing an increasingly comprehensive picture of the role of women in our rich and varied history.

Such books on groups of women are essential, but books that focus on the lives of individuals are equally indispensable. Biographies can be inspirational, offering their readers the example of people with vision who have looked outside themselves for their goals and have often struggled against great obstacles to achieve them. Marian Anderson, for instance, had to overcome racial bigotry in order to perfect her art and perform as a concert singer. Isadora Duncan defied the rules of classical dance to find true artistic freedom. Jane Addams had to break down society's notions of the proper role for women in order to create new social situations, notably the settlement house. All of these women had to come to terms both with themselves and with the world in which they lived. Only then could they move ahead as pioneers in their chosen callings.

Biography can inspire not only by adulation but also by realism. It helps us to see not only the qualities in others that we hope to emulate, but also, perhaps, the weaknesses that made them "human." By helping us identify with the subject on a more personal level they help us feel that we, too, can achieve such goals. We read about Eleanor Roosevelt, for instance, who occupied a unique and seemingly enviable position as the wife of the president. Yet we can sympathize with her inner dilemma; an inherently shy woman, she had to force herself to live a most public life in order to use her position to benefit others. We may not be able to imagine ourselves having the immense poetic talent of Emily Dickinson, but from her story we can understand the challenges faced by a creative woman who was expected to fulfill many family responsibilities. And though few of us will ever reach the level of athletic accomplishment displayed by Wilma Rudolph or Babe Zaharias, we can still appreciate their spirit, their overwhelming will to excel.

A biography is a multifaceted lens. It is first of all a magnification, the intimate examination of one particular life. But at the same time, it is a wide-angle lens, informing us about the world in which the subject lived. We come away from reading about one life knowing more about the social, political, and economic fabric of the time. It is for this reason, perhaps, that the great New England essayist Ralph Waldo Emerson wrote in 1841, "There is properly no history: only biography." And it is also why biography, and particularly women's biography, will continue to fascinate writers and readers alike.

Abigail Van Buren (left) and Ann Landers attend their 50th high school reunion in Sioux City, Iowa, in 1986. Despite a long and public falling-out, the twin advice columnists say they remain close.

1

DEAR ANN, DEAR ABBY

Dear Abby: I just can't believe that you took the time to write a personal letter. And when you said, "Please write again. I care," I cried.

Abby, why would anyone want to help me straighten out my rotten mixed-up life? I don't deserve it. Five times people saved me from suicide. Sometimes I wish they'd have let me die—it's so hard to keep saying 'thank you.'

I'm a registered nurse and should be helping people, but instead people are helping me. I feel so guilty.

I have a fantastic new psychiatrist who acts as though he really cares about me. I don't know why anyone would care if I lived or died. I'm not pretty or smart or productive. I'm a burden and a problem to everyone who knows me. But this doctor makes me feel so great.

Is life worth living to feel great for only one hour a week? Help me.

—Finished at Twenty-Four

Dear Finished at Twenty-Four: You're far from finished, you're just beginning to realize how precious life is. Every human being who reaches out for help wants it—and deserves it. It's always darkest just *before dawn. Hang in there and don't let your doctor (or yourself) down. You can make it if you try. I'm counting on you.*

●   ●   ●

Dear Ann Landers: A man (12 years my junior) talks of marriage, but his conversations all wind up with questions about my financial situation. I've been warned that he is insincere. If this is true, why does he swear he worships the ground I walk on?

—Miss B. L. K.

Dear Miss B. L. K.: He probably thinks there's oil under it.

●   ●   ●

Dear Abby: I've been married to a good-looking cross-country truck driver for ten years. I'm not the suspicious type, but Friday night he came off the road with two long scratches on his left hip. They were fairly deep scratches. Yet neither his shorts nor his trousers were ripped.

When I asked him where he got the scratches, he said they were probably from a feather in the bed. Now, Abby, I'd like to believe him, but do they still have feather bedding in modern motels? And could anybody get scratched like this from a feather?

—Not Dumb

Dear Not: It's unlikely that the scratches came from a feather. It was probably the whole chick.

●   ●   ●

Ann Landers and Abigail Van Buren (or "Dear Abby") have been answering letters like these for more than four decades. To the confused and the lonely—like

"Dejected in Denver" and "Bummed Out in Boston"—to nearly 200 million people all over the world who regularly read their widely syndicated newspaper columns, Ann and Abby are wise, witty friends.

Ann and Abby dominate the advice column business, and they have for more than 40 years. They serve as free psychiatrists, voices of reason, and standard-bearers of social normalcy. Using direct and simple language, the twin advice columnists confirm the values of our society and constantly update their own responses to reflect the changes it undergoes. Both columns articulate and shape our shared moral conscience.

Even though readers may not always agree with what Dear Ann and Dear Abby say, they keep reading them. Maybe those of us who do are trying to understand what our most common problems are and to find out what conventional wisdom says we should do to solve them. We may read Ann and Abby because their

Popo Phillips poses in front of her typewriter shortly after she began writing as Abigail Van Buren in 1956. Even today, the woman best known as "Abby" says she can't wait to get to work each morning.

At her home in Chicago, Eppie Lederer sifts through the piles of mail her "Ann Landers" column generates. Eppie began her career as an advice columnist only 89 days before her twin began writing the "Dear Abby" column.

columns are about sex or about unfaithfulness. Or we may read them to learn about the rules that govern the way people interact with one another. But we also turn to Ann Landers and Abigail Van Buren simply to get a good laugh.

To their faithful readers, Ann Landers and Abigail Van Buren are sincere and gutsy advisors who provide down-home guidance in a reassuring manner that generates trust. They are snappy and sensible; their witty and wise words appear in nearly 2,000 newspapers and are translated into as many as 20 languages. Their views, which are mostly a mixture of liberal politics and conservative morals (such as their shared belief that a woman "owns her own body" but should "save" it for her future husband), are almost identical on most important issues. With their bright eyes, arched eyebrows, and stiff bouffant hairdos—including their trademark pointy sideflips (Ann's to the left and Abby's to the right)—the two newspaper columnists look surprisingly similar as well.

Or not so surprisingly, considering the fact that Ann Landers and Abigail Van Buren are sisters—twin sisters. And they are the most famous, most widely recognized twins of the 20th century. In the four decades that they have written their columns, Ann, Abby, or both have been consistently included on lists naming the most admired or most important women in the United States. No other sisters or twins have ever appeared on these lists, and no other women have remained on these lists over such an extended period.

Together, Ann Landers and Abigail Van Buren receive as many as 15,000 letters weekly. A single column by either one can generate 100,000 letters of response. Despite the fact that they turned 80 in 1998, the twin columnists both continue to work at least eight hours a day, answering all of their own letters and typing their daily columns on electric typewriters. Neither claims to think about retiring. "I don't know what I'd do with my time if I wasn't working," Van Buren told *People* magazine in 1998. "My job isn't a burden to me; it really is a pleasure. I can't wait to get to work in the morning." Her energetic sister, meanwhile, aims to continue her popular column indefinitely: "I plan to die at the typewriter. Just keel over at the machine," says Landers.

To millions of readers, the twins are Ann Landers and Dear Abby, the reigning queens of what used to be called "lonely hearts" columns. In real life, however, they are Esther Pauline Friedman Lederer, or "Eppie," and Pauline Esther Friedman Phillips, or "Popo."

Eppie Friedman was born just 17 minutes before

Popo. Eppie became Ann Landers in 1955, only 89 days before Popo transformed herself into Abigail Van Buren. But Popo published two books of her collected columns before Eppie saw her first "Ann Landers" collection in print. (Each has now published seven books.) And Popo owned her column—and her pen name—from the start. Only after 30 years was Eppie given full legal rights to Ann Landers's works.

When the Friedman twins were young, they looked and dressed exactly alike. They always double-dated, and they were wed in a double-marriage ceremony two days before their 21st birthday. Until they became Ann and Abby, Eppie and Popo were extremely close, almost like mirror images of one another. They were virtually inseparable as children and best friends while they were both young housewives and new mothers.

After the sisters became famous, their normal sibling rivalry turned bitter, and their rift was widely publicized. After an eight-year period during which Eppie and Popo refused to speak to one another, the sisters managed to forge a truce and agreed not to discuss their work with each other. As Ann Landers and Dear Abby, the sisters have continued their cutthroat competition, however, with an occasional public flare-up of their long-running feud.

Yet, because the twins agree on almost everything they discuss in their columns, the newspaper-reading public often confuses the two. At American dinner tables and beside office water coolers, one might hear the following: "I read it in 'Ann Landers.' Or was it 'Dear Abby'?" The careful reader may note that Ann Landers (Eppie) tends to run longer columns and often dwells on more serious topics than Abby (Popo) does, or that Abby's columns are usually more humorous and contain more snappy one-liners than those of Ann Landers.

Although they still look very much alike, Eppie recently went blonde, and when Popo is feeling especially competitive, she will point out that Eppie's nose job and other cosmetic surgeries are responsible for the differences in their appearances. Both sisters are in admirable shape, each weighing in at a slim 110 pounds. They are both 5' 2", and neither one looks her age.

The most influential twins in history are not college graduates; nor are they trained in social work, counseling, or journalism. "When I started writing the column at thirty-seven, I thought I was worldly and sophisticated. . . . Let me tell you, I didn't know anything," admits Eppie. Both sisters have learned a great deal on the job. But each of them also has a gift for knowing what topics will interest readers and what advice might help their correspondents. When unsure about how to handle a problem, neither sister hesitates to call on a professional expert. "I'm not an authority on anything," Eppie states candidly, "but I tap the best brains in the country."

Both columnists tend to avoid specific advice and prefer to refer readers to their priests and ministers, local social service agencies, or self-help organizations such as Alcoholics Anonymous and Al-Anon. They share the opinion that most people, if they can articulate their problems and are offered a bit of guidance, are capable of working out their difficulties themselves. Yet the sisters understand the awesome extent of their special responsibilities as advisors to troubled people. As Eppie has explained, "The responsibility is there for the taking. There is an enormous need for such a column, and I view it as one of journalism's great challenges, a unique opportunity to spotlight ignorance, fear, and stupidity. I pray only that I am equal to the task." Popo says, "I don't force my views on other people. I feel very strongly about people telling other people how to live. . . . I think people should be able to make up their own minds."

As writers, Eppie and Popo both use a style that is down-to-earth, rich with wisecracks and puns, and often painfully pointed. Dear Abby has advised, "A bad habit never disappears miraculously; it's an undo-it-yourself project." Ann Landers frequently suggests the following method for dealing with someone (including oneself) who needs to be mildly rebuked: "Forty lashes with a wet noodle." Landers's favorite admonishment, "Wake up and smell the coffee," has become a household expression in America; few people who hear it require an explanation. Popo has attributed the enduring success of her own and her sister's columns to their similarly saucy style. "People like something that's cute and flip. It might be the only laugh they get all day," she once told the trade journal *Editor & Publisher*.

Eppie and Popo's ready senses of humor may also explain why the two columnists have not experienced depression or despair from reading the daily deluge of letters from pregnant teenagers, jilted lovers, abused spouses of alcoholics, and ever-younger drug addicts. From their first seasons as columnists, both Ann and Abby vigilantly avoided suffering the same gloomy fate as the infamous Miss Lonelyhearts, the title character and protagonist of Nathanael West's classic 1933 novel.

Miss Lonelyhearts is the tale of a male newspaper journalist, dubbed "Miss Lonelyhearts," who is assigned to write a daily "agony column" of advice for troubled readers. Unable to remain detached from his woeful correspondents, the journalist spirals into a pattern of excessive drinking, violence, adultery, depression, and finally madness. Near the conclusion of this short, dark novel, Miss Lonelyhearts describes himself as "the rock." West says of his main character, "He did not feel guilty. He did not feel."

In her early days as Ann Landers, Eppie read the poignant West novel, which her concerned editor had provided. "I never could become like the columnist in *Miss Lonelyhearts*. I'm too strong and confident," she stated. Some time later, a more experienced Ann Landers reflected, "I have learned how it is with the stumbling, tortured people in this world who have nobody to talk

to. . . . No situation, I now realize, is too bizarre, too idiotic, or too risky to be real. Somebody, somewhere, will do anything if he or she is lonely enough, desperate enough, or pushed beyond the threshold of tolerance." In 1995, when a journalist for the *New Yorker* noticed the copy of *Miss Lonelyhearts* resting on Eppie's bookshelf in her study, she answered, "You have to insulate yourself against what is coming at you. Otherwise, you go right to pieces. I've had some letters that are very, very sad. And hopeless. . . . What do you tell them? What do you say to those people?"

In one of her best-selling books, a collection of her columns called *The Best of Dear Abby*, Popo acknowledges West's novel as a literary masterpiece, but points out what she believes is the novel's flaw: the author,

One of the predecessors of the "Ann Landers" and "Dear Abby" newspaper columns was "Dorothy Dix Talks," written by Elizabeth Meriweather Gilmer, shown here in 1940. Gilmer's column first appeared locally in Louisiana before the turn of the 20th century; it was so successful that she became the first advice columnist in the United States to earn a national audience.

and therefore the protagonist, "forgot the saving grace of humor," she declares. Abigail Van Buren remembers to laugh while she works. She notes that "a tougher-minded Miss Lonelyhearts, one who could laugh and bring healing laughter to his sorry clients" would have survived, although the story might have been ruined. "It made a great novel. But I couldn't have written it," Abby has told her readers. "I take the view that not only is it good for us to laugh at the more absurd letter writers, it's good for them, too. Sometimes it's shock treatment. It helps get a problem into perspective once it's cut down to a size that can be managed."

Throughout history, plenty of people have been willing to take on the daunting task of advising others on how to improve their lives. In 1855, the London *Journal* ran a lovelorn column in which one female correspondent was ominously warned, "You must be cautious. Your lover evidently does not respect his future bride. The asp lurks beneath the flowers." In the late 1920s, lovelorn columns aimed at women readers became popular in American newspapers. The first of these to garner a national audience was called "Dorothy Dix Talks." Originally authored by Mrs. Elizabeth Meriweather Gilmer, the column first appeared locally in New Orleans's *Times-Picayune* around 1896. By the start of the Second World War, "Dorothy Dix Talks" was featured in 300 newspapers and reached about 60 million readers. Mrs. Marie Manning Gasch's column, which she wrote for the Hearst chain of newspapers under the pen name Beatrice Fairfax, was also quite popular at that time. Obviously, the Miss Lonelyhearts–style newspaper column, which provided wise and moral counsel for the troubles of individual readers, had found a place in modern American culture.

When the "Ann Landers" and "Dear Abby" columns first appeared in the mid-1950s, the Dorothy Dix column, then written by Muriel Agnelli, had become one

of two competing national columns. The other was written by Mary Haworth. Although Eppie and Popo were not the first lovelorn columnists to achieve worldwide popularity, they were remarkably different from their predecessors. From their earliest days on the job, Ann Landers and Abigail Van Buren asked to be called "advice columnists" rather than lovelorn columnists. They believed that the old moniker does not adequately define the "Ann Landers" and "Dear Abby" columns, which include letters dealing with a much wider spectrum of problems than broken hearts and which give voice to politically "hot" issues, including homosexuality, sexually transmitted diseases, birth control, abortion, and social tolerance.

But their columns are also entertaining. Ann and Abby tend to write "cute and flip" responses, and their columns are often laugh-out-loud funny. Their witty responses to letters have earned them phenomenally large followings. Their columns created a new style in

Oprah Winfrey speaks with First Lady Hillary Clinton in a 1995 episode of The Oprah Winfrey Show. *Some observers suggest that the highly popular advice columns of Ann Landers and Abigail Van Buren gave rise to talk-show TV programs like Winfrey's.*

journalism advice and ushered in the current era of confessional tell-alls as media entertainment. In a 1993 conversation with Ann Landers, *Psychology Today* pointed to "shows like 'Oprah' [*The Oprah Winfrey Show*] as the offspring of your column."

How alike are Eppie Lederer and Ann Landers, or Popo Phillips and Abigail Van Buren? "Refer to me as Ann Landers," Eppie tells interviewers who ask whether they are talking to Ann or Eppie. "Actually, they are one and the same." She sees herself as "a listener, a helper," and views her international fame and popularity with the humble eye of a true humanitarian: "All the column means to me is an extraordinary opportunity to do good in the world."

Popo, too, is an acknowledged do-gooder. "I have always gravitated toward people with problems," she has explained of her many years of charity work, volunteerism, and "Dear Abby" columns. She enjoys helping others because, she says, "People are so grateful for any help that you can give them." Like her sister, Popo prefers to be called by her professional name—Abby—and she has trademarked the name Abigail Van Buren so that only she can use it legally.

In real life the twins claim to be close, yet the competition between columnists Ann and Abby is ongoing. Every year, the sisters share near-equal billing in their extra-lengthy entries in *Who's Who in America*, in which they both list the dozens of awards and honors they've received, some from the same universities and organizations. Each of their newspaper syndicates continues to boast that its respective column is printed in the same number of newspapers (about 1,200 each) and reaches the same number of readers (about 90 million per syndicate). Creators Syndicate, which handles the "Ann Landers" column, brags that Ann is "the most widely read columnist in the world." Universal Press, Abby's syndicate, claims that research has proven that Abigail Van Buren is "the most widely syndicated advice columnist in the world." *The Best of Dear Abby* labels Abigail Van Buren as "America's most popular advice columnist." *Wake Up and Smell the Coffee*, Ann Landers's most recent collection of columns, calls her "the most popular columnist in the United States" and "the most trusted woman in America."

No matter which one may have more column space *this* week, both Eppie and Popo have led lives of extraordinary accomplishment. To millions of people around the world, Ann and Abby seem like their own sisters. They personify generosity and human kindness, and they reaffirm the virtues of good and proper behavior. After years of unprecedented popularity, Ann Landers and Abigail Van Buren have become American institutions. As Popo points out, "Eppie and I must be doing something right. There must be some reason we're still here."

A wise Greek philosopher once said, "Nature gave us one tongue, but two ears . . . so we may hear twice as much as we speak." Ann Landers and Abigail Van Buren have been listening twice as carefully as they have been speaking for eight decades. Even as precocious children, the feisty and outspoken Friedman twins were uncannily adept at "telling it like it is." From the start, Eppie and Popo were special, a pair of originals, always twice the fun.

Encouraged to behave as stereotypical twins, Pauline "Popo" (above) and Esther "Eppie" Friedman not only dressed identically, but they also shared the same interests and friends. They were so alike as children and teenagers that years later, Eppie's daughter would write that "Mother broke her arm when she was eleven; Popo thought it happened to her."

2

EPPIE AND POPO

Dear Ann Landers: I have twin girls, two years old. Please forgive a mother's pride, but they are pretty and loaded with personality. Of course, they attract a great deal of attention
wherever they go. People stare, poke each other with elbows and
say, "Look at the twins." My daughters are aware of the furor they
create and revel in it.

How did you and your twin, Dear Abby, react to the staring, whis-
pering and finger-pointing when you were growing up? Was it annoy-
ing? Was it fun? Did it have any impact on the way you thought about
yourselves? Did it make you more reclusive or more outgoing?

What advice do you have for a mother who is trying to raise twin
girls to be normal, well-adjusted human beings?

—H. H. U. in Miami

Dear Miami: My sister and I were almost always the center of
attention from the day we were born. . . . Since our mother dressed us
alike from infancy until we were married (a double wedding, of
course, with identical gowns and bridal veils), no one could miss us.

The wonderful thing about being a twin is that you are never

Popo (left) and Eppie as 13-year-olds growing up in Sioux City, Iowa. The lively, pretty twins earned extra attention by learning to perform songs and skits for family and friends.

lonely. . . . The awful part of being a twin is that you are never alone. There was no opportunity for quiet introspection and honest self-appraisal. Granted, the "togetherness" was great fun, but it denied us the opportunity to develop as individuals. We would never escape the image of the sister act.

In retrospect, we grew up surprisingly unspoiled, although we traded on our twinship shamelessly, a natural and easy thing to do. We also got into a great deal of mischief. What one couldn't think of the other one could.

My advice to mothers of twins is this: Do not, repeat not, dress your twins alike. Treat them as individuals, not halves of a single unit. Encourage them to have different friends. If possible, send them to different schools. If that isn't possible, try to put them in different classes.

Do not make your twins feel guilty if they fail to stick together on all issues. Encourage them to be independent and have their own point of view.

Be impartial, and always remain neutral when they have their battles. Don't take sides. . . . Be aware that sib-

ling rivalry is natural and with twins it is intensified.

Not until my daughter Margo was born did I realize what a remarkable (and heroic) woman my mother was. I have thought many times that God must have a special place at his right hand for the mother of twins. Especially if the twins are anything like my sister and me.

●   ●   ●

On July 4, 1918, Eppie and Popo Friedman were born in Sioux City, Iowa, the heart of the Midwest. Their parents, Abraham and Rebecca, were Russian Jews who had arrived in America in 1908 and who spoke both Russian and Yiddish fluently. Anti-Semitism was rife in the small, rough city, in part because a Jewish racketeering mob called the Syndicate sold illegal liquor bootlegged from Canada during the period known as Prohibition, when alcohol was outlawed in the United States. But most Jewish families in Sioux City attempted to battle the bigotry they faced by leading staid and morally exemplary lives.

The twins rounded out the Friedman family to four girls (a brother had died in infancy). As little girls, the twins both wore their coal-black hair short, with bangs that highlighted their sparkling blue eyes. They were peppy, pretty, and bright, and they were never apart from one another.

Because most people viewed the two girls as a unit, the sisters were raised to see themselves as one. According to Eppie's daughter, Margo Howard, who wrote a biography of her mother in 1982 called *Eppie,* there was even confusion about what specific events happened to which twin. "Their selfhood was blurry because their real identity came from being twins," she wrote. "They would tell each other's stories, and in their minds their lives became interchangeable."

Although the sisters did not look *exactly* alike—Eppie was a little taller and thinner, and she had dimples—

most people could never tell them apart. The girls' violin teacher was one of these confused individuals, and the twins took advantage of the situation: on the days Eppie was unprepared for her lesson, Popo, the more able musician, would take two lessons in a row—one as herself, and the second posing as her sister.

The twins shared not only a bedroom but also the same bed. Until the day they married, Eppie and Popo slept side by side, often with their arms wrapped around each other. When they were 13, their parents bought them a set of twin beds, but the girls tucked a violin case under the blankets of one bed and slept together in the other.

In school, at the insistence of their parents, the girls were assigned to all of the same classes. When enlightened teachers at their junior high school recommended that they be separated, the twins told the principal that they would "rather die" than be apart.

Encouraged to appear the same in every detail, Eppie and Popo were also pressured to conform to one another's most trivial personality characteristics. "I remember the sense of guilt I suffered when, at the age of eleven, I screwed up the courage to express a preference for Shredded Wheat over Puffed Rice," Eppie recalled as an adult. "I had been brought up to feel that everything with twins should be alike."

Abe Friedman, or A. B., as everyone called him, was uneducated, unskilled, and penniless when he arrived in Sioux City in 1910. After years of peddling chickens from a pushcart, he bought a grocery store. He was well loved in the Russian immigrant neighborhood, where he was known for his generosity in helping other struggling families by allowing them to buy groceries on credit in his store.

When the twins were in their early teens, A. B. bought a vaudeville-movie theater called the World, located in downtown Sioux City. The family moved into a two-story house about 20 blocks from the theater.

A. B. quickly purchased three more theaters, including the Orpheum, Sioux City's center for "high class vaude-ville and the best feature photoplays," according to a 1987 biography of Ann Landers and Abigail Van Buren, *Dear Ann, Dear Abby.* He then took shares in a variety of other businesses, including an apartment house, an ice factory, and a beer distributorship. He also began to get involved in civic works and community affairs. He lent money to people in need, and he even sent his movie projectionist to show free movies on Sundays at a home for unmarried pregnant teens.

A. B.'s kindness deeply impressed his youngest girls. According to granddaughter Margo, "Success to A. B. was simple: it meant doing well and doing good. Mak-ing money, and giving some of it away." The girls' mother was also an unusually generous woman.

Abigail Van Buren displays a photograph of her beloved parents, Abraham (A. B.) and Rebecca Friedman. The couple emigrated from Russia to the United States in 1908, where they raised their four children. Van Buren remembers her child-hood as being "rich with love." Her twin sister recalls that both parents were warm, giving people who never turned down those in need. "Our house was always full of guests," Ann Landers has said.

"Becky," a diminutive woman who stood 5' 3" in heels, fed and housed a number of homeless people who knocked on her door during the lean years of the Depression, and she opened her home to all of the lonely out-of-town show business performers who played at A. B.'s theaters. Popo recalls their childhood as being "rich with love. We never heard our mother call our father Abraham. And he never addressed her as Rebecca. It was always Darling, Sweetheart, or Dear." According to Eppie, "My father was the sort of man people came to for advice. My mother couldn't turn away anyone with a hard-luck story. Our house was always full of guests."

The Friedman home was also rich with humor, music, and dancing. The twins would sing and dance for their many eclectic visitors. Because they were raised by parents who were always helping others, the twins wanted to do good, too. At 10 years old, they offered to play their violins for the prisoners of the county jail. They sang at hospitals, and they shared their bag lunches with children whose families were less fortunate than their own. "Be a *mensch*," Becky would tell her children, using the Yiddish word for a person of integrity and honor. "Be a real person."

When the Friedman twins began attending Central High School in 1932, they made a striking pair. Petite, attractive, and well dressed, the sisters sported identical wraps of black-and-white "civet cat," the only fur coats in the school. They often showed up at parties sharing a single pocketbook—and the same escort. "Together they were a four-legged attention-getting device," Margo declares in the biography of her mother. Eppie recalled, "We were side by side in every class, confusing the teachers, overwhelming the boys, antagonizing the girls, and playing the double exposure for all it was worth."

Sometimes the teen duo used music to win over their teachers, making up ditties to explain why their grades had slipped. The Friedman twins were constantly creating poems, parodies, and witty letters as well, and they were never at a loss for words. "We had the edge," boasts Popo. "When the school orchestra went to the state music contest, we were the girls the photographers always picked out."

Boys always picked out the Friedman twins, too. When they turned 16 and began dating, the girls went to their father's theater employees for information and guidance. Their interest in sex, however, was as conventional as the widely held values of the era. "All the nice little Jewish girls in Sioux City got married and had a family. A woman's role was to raise the babies, keep house, and be a useful and dutiful companion to her husband," Eppie says about that period.

The girls dated Christians as well as boys of their own faith—behavior that was regarded as lib-

eral at the time. But neither twin smoked cigarettes or drank alcohol, and their togetherness provided enough built-in sexual restraint that they managed to stay out of trouble in that regard.

Enrolled in the general high school curriculum, the sisters took typing classes as well as college prep courses. When they graduated in 1936, they chose to attend Morningside College, a Methodist school in Sioux City.

In college, the Friedman twins were very popular, and as always, they commanded attention. Dressed in identical black-and-white striped furs, the sisters attended the same classes, including a journalism course

One of A. B. Friedman's many business ventures involved Sioux City's Orpheum Theater, shown here in an early photograph. From A. B., Eppie and Popo learned to look out for others who were less fortunate than they were: each weekend, A. B. sent his projectionist to show free movies to residents of a home for single pregnant teens.

Eppie and Popo Friedman in a Morningside College yearbook photo from 1937. While in college, the popular and mischievous twins launched a gossip column called "Campus Rats" that exposed campus secrets and chronicled various events.

that they chose because the teacher was reputed to be an easy grader. They submitted a sample gossip column to the school newspaper, the *Collegian Reporter*, and before long a weekly column called "Campus Rats" appeared in the paper, carrying the byline "By the Friedman Twins."

"Campus Rats" was a kind of "spy" column that tattled on such school goings-on as secretive romances and visits to saloons or to theaters showing "art films" about nudist colonies. Although Eppie and Popo's scoops generated trouble for some students and often poked fun at the most visible personalities on campus, it was the favorite column of most people.

In those days, the fraternity weekends hosted by colleges were *the* social events for coeds. The popular Friedman twins received lots of invitations from college boys and, because their father could afford to send them, they traveled to various universities attended by

Sioux City's most eligible bachelors. On a visit to the University of Minnesota while they were still in high school, Popo had met Morton Phillips, the son of one of the wealthiest families in Minnesota. She dated this heir to a multimillion-dollar liquor fortune for three years, continuing to go on double dates with Eppie.

During wintertime breaks from school, the twins traveled to California and Florida with their parents. During their junior year at Morningside College, while on vacation in southern California, Eppie met a law student from the University of California at Los Angeles. Smart and ambitious, Lewis Dreyer was the son of a vice president at RKO Pictures, a film company. After a brief courtship, Eppie and Lewis became engaged. Since Popo and Mort Phillips were also engaged by this time, the four planned a double wedding ceremony for the summer of 1939.

After announcing their engagements, however, the Friedman twins decided to drop out of Morningside at the end of their junior year. They quickly jettisoned the popular "Campus Rats" column, the attentive frat boys, and the beginnings of a formal education in favor of the more conventional future both sisters admittedly desired. The Friedman twins wanted nothing more than to be wives and homemakers.

While shopping for their wedding veils in a local boutique, the twins were carefully attended by the buyer for the ladies' hats department. He seemed to be especially interested in Eppie. Blond and handsome, the young sales clerk struck both sisters as being very bright and quite appealing. While Eppie was trying on veils, Jules Lederer took Popo aside and confided that he wished to ask Eppie to a dance but felt awkward about doing so since she was engaged. "Ask her anyhow," advised Popo. "All she can say is no."

Eppie did not say no, even when Jules announced, "You're the first girl I ever met that I wanted to marry . . . and you're coming in to buy a wedding veil."

Jules quickly charmed the rest of the Friedman family, and shortly after Eppie's first date with him she realized that she could not marry Lewis Dreyer. With the support of her family, Eppie returned her engagement ring and the double wedding was canceled. But it wasn't long before Jules asked Eppie to marry him. With the new groom gracefully substituted, the double wedding was rescheduled for July 2, 1939.

Although Eppie had turned down a law student from a rich family for a salesman with little more than a charming smile, she knew she had picked a winner. Jules Lederer had dropped out of high school in Detroit to help support his large family when his father, a traveling salesman, died in a car accident. By the time he was 19, Jules was a department store manager of millinery (women's hats) in Lansing, Michigan. At 21, he was promoted and transferred to Sioux City. Lederer was ambitious and experienced—and he was crazy about Eppie. "The boy's got potential," A. B. announced after meeting his future son-in-law. Eppie's heart told her that she'd chosen the right man.

As always, the twins were together, dressed in identical outfits, when they walked down the aisle of the Shaare Zion Synagogue in Sioux City with A. B. between them. In their white gowns of heavy satin with dramatic veils that flowed from satin and seed pearl headpieces, the brides dazzled their guests. Each bride wore a single strand of pearls and carried white orchids. There were two maids of honor, two groomsmen, seven bridesmaids, and seven ushers in the wedding party, plus three rabbis—one Orthodox, one Conservative, and one Reform. While 200 guests attended the ceremony, a crowd of more than 100 more gathered outside the synagogue, kept under control by policemen on horseback. Practically everyone in town, it seemed, wanted to get a glimpse of the beautiful twin brides.

After the lengthy ceremony, 750 friends and relatives attended the festive reception at the Martin Hotel in downtown Sioux City. One guest told the local paper afterward that "even for a slightly theatrical family, the Friedmans outdid themselves."

Of course, a double honeymoon followed while the twins postponed their ultimate separation for a few more days. The first stop on their two-week tour was the Edgewater Beach Hotel on the shores of Lake Michigan in Chicago. There, Jules promptly ran out of money, so the Lederers returned to Sioux City to their one-bedroom apartment, while the Phillipses continued on to Banff, Lake Louise, and other Canadian destinations before settling in Minneapolis, Minnesota.

Mrs. Morton Phillips—no longer viewed as one-half of the Friedman twins—embarked on her new life as the privileged wife of an up-and-coming young executive from an extremely wealthy family. Mrs. Jules Lederer and her new husband, on the other hand, were $300 in debt. For the first time in their lives, the twins had made significantly different choices. And, for the first time in their 21 years, the twins were living apart from one another.

Mrs. Jules Lederer (Eppie) as the new Ann Landers. With her husband working long hours, Eppie embarked on her career as an advice columnist while searching for a way to "serve, to do something for someone else."

3

FROM "EPPIE" TO ANN LANDERS

> "*Trouble is the great equalizer. It doesn't make any difference who you are, or what you have, when you and your neighbor share the same problem you become brothers and sisters under the skin.*"
>
> —*Ann Landers in* Who's Who in America

The new Mrs. Lederer had a lot to learn about the details involved in keeping house. Since the twins were several years younger than their two more responsible sisters, and because their mother was a full-time, devoted housewife, Eppie had gained little experience in cooking, cleaning, doing laundry, or paying bills. As a newlywed, she even boiled lamb chops once by mistake! But she had plenty of time to develop her skills, managing the household on very little money while Jules tried to make a living as a salesman.

"In the beginning of my married life, I lived with no luxuries at all," Eppie recounts. "We had no extra money for anything." Jules was earning $35 a week, and he sent $10 weekly to his mother and siblings in Detroit. The newlyweds' tiny two-room apartment grew even more crowded after baby Margo arrived in March 1940.

A family celebration: Eppie (right) and her husband, Jules Lederer, at the 1962 wedding of their daughter, Margo (left). According to Margo's biography of her mother, Jules and Eppie's own marriage was very happy. "Nothing seemed tough," she wrote, "it just seemed like fun."

To expand his sales opportunities and increase the family's meager income, Jules had to relocate frequently. Within the next few years, the Lederers left Sioux City for St. Louis, Missouri, returned to Sioux City, and then relocated to New Orleans, Louisiana, before settling in Milwaukee, Wisconsin. Every time they moved, Jules began working longer hours. "I saw more of a moving van than I saw of my husband," recalls Eppie.

According to Margo, her parents' memories of their early years together were fond ones: "Nothing seemed tough, it just seemed like fun." Even though Eppie Lederer had been the pampered daughter of a successful businessman, she quickly learned how to meet her own family's needs on a decidedly skimpy budget. "Doing without, together, never hurt anyone," she declared.

While the Lederers lived in New Orleans, Eppie worked for the American Red Cross as a "Gray Lady" volunteer at a naval hospital. The Second World War had come to America when Japan bombed the naval base at Pearl Harbor, Hawaii, on December 7, 1941. Sociable as ever, Eppie enjoyed her hours as a Gray Lady, and she soon met the first of her life-changing mentors.

Dr. Robert Stolar was a dermatologist (skin disease specialist) at the hospital where Eppie volunteered. She invited the intelligent, engaging bachelor home for dinner and to meet Jules, who enjoyed Stolar and began calling him "the derm." When Eppie brought her new friend into the family nursery to say hello to two-year-old Margo, the excited baby jumped up and down in her crib and pulled down her pants. Eppie was appalled and scolded Margo, calling her "naughty-naughty, bad-bad."

Stolar advised Eppie that her reprimand was too severe and could cause the little girl to regard her own body as shameful. When Eppie mentioned that Margo stuttered and suffered from asthma, a respiratory illness that can have psychological origins, the doctor admonished Eppie. "Well, of course she does!" he said. "You're making her crazy."

Eppie Lederer listened to her soft-spoken friend. He was kind and well educated, and she trusted him. Stolar became an important confidant, not only for Eppie but also, as years went by, for Jules and Margo. He had developed an intuitive understanding that many of the skin diseases he treated stemmed from emotional or psychological difficulties. Margo, who began referring to Stolar as the "Answer Man," credits him with the mind-over-matter cure of her asthma when she was 13 years old. She also attributes the development of Eppie's singular and eventually world-renowned identity to the gentle, far-reaching interventions of Dr. Stolar.

"The derm" supported her through another kind of change as well. According to him, Eppie Lederer had plastic surgery on her nose—an uncommon and extravagant undertaking at that time—because she wished for a more classic appearance. According to Eppie, however, she had the surgery to repair a deviated septum (an abnormality of the membrane separating the two halves of the nasal passage). Whatever the reason, the surgical alteration resulted in an indisputable change: Eppie no longer looked exactly like her sister. After 25 years of having an interchangeable identity, the twins were no longer identical in appearance.

In 1944, Jules was drafted into the army and sent to Little Rock, Arkansas. Coincidentally, Popo's husband, Mort, was stationed there as well. The two men became close friends, forming a bond that lasted for 30 years.

Eppie and little Margo were living with the Friedmans in Sioux City, waiting out Jules's tour of duty, when 56-year-old Becky Friedman suffered a fatal cerebral hemorrhage. Popo and Eppie supported one another in their grief, and their husbands, who went on emergency leave from the service upon their mother-in-law's death, had a chance to observe for the first time the unusually close bond shared by their wives.

When the two men were released from the army in 1945, Mort Phillips offered Jules Lederer a job and Jules accepted. The Lederers moved to Los Angeles, where Jules sold cookware for a Phillips-owned company called Guardian Service. Working 14 hours a day and seven days a week, Jules traveled door-to-door and demonstrated a unique line of steam-heat cookware by preparing dinners for families and their guests in their own homes. Eppie pitched in by preparing vegetables, helping to serve the meals, and then washing the pots

and pans whenever Jules's assistants failed to show up—
which was frequently. "A lot of women would have
resented this, but not me," Eppie stated later. "You see,
this was my contribution to Jules's success."

When Jules was promoted to district sales manager
for Guardian later that year, the Lederers moved to
Chicago's South Side. Eppie set up a card table in their
living room and sent out funny poems to friends, calling them "Eppie-grams." Six months later, Jules was
named vice president of sales for Guardian's parent
company, National Presto Industries. Mort had just
been promoted to executive vice president of Presto,
where his father was chairman of the board.

The Phillips family moved to Eau Claire, Wisconsin,
the headquarters of Presto, one of the town's major
employers. The Lederers joined them there a few weeks
later. Eppie reveled in her new position as the wife of an
executive. She entertained guests in the tiny dining
room of her little white house and enjoyed dressing up
for dinners at local clubs and restaurants. Since Jules's
executive position entailed a great deal of time on the
road, she also had to find new ways to amuse herself.
Her husband's typical workweek of 60 to 80 hours
taught Eppie "how to be alone without feeling sorry
for myself."

Margo recalls how her mother drove her to school
every day dressed in "a floor-length nightie, fuzzy slippers, and a knee-length mink coat." One morning,
Eppie was stopped for speeding. The arresting officer
sent her to the police station, fuzzy slippers and all, but
Eppie managed to talk her way out of a ticket. Eppie's
poor driving skills were widely recognized in the town
of 32,000—one irate neighbor cracked a rake across her
windshield as she sped past his house.

Popo and Eppie enjoyed their time together in Eau
Claire. They went on shopping expeditions by train to
Illinois and Minneapolis, and they displayed their fine
taste in fashion at numerous community and civic

Dr. Robert Stolar, variously called the "Answer Man" and "the derm" by the Lederers, became a valued confidant not only of Eppie but also of Jules and Margo. The soft-spoken dermatologist is credited with having fostered Eppie's identity as Ann Landers.

events. The twins frequently visited their father, A. B., at the Mayo Clinic in Rochester, Minnesota, where he stayed until his death from cancer in 1953. Both worked as Gray Ladies at the local hospital, continuing the Friedman family tradition of doing good for others.

Eppie, who liked organizing, soon became active in the National Council of Christians and Jews, helping to raise funds and plan joint charitable events to increase cooperation among people of both faiths. She worked hard to establish a League of Women Voters branch in Eau Claire, and she published her first newspaper editorial on the need for community involvement in service organizations. During this time she become an avid newspaper reader herself, intent on keeping up with local and world affairs.

By 1950, Eppie was heavily involved in local politics and had launched a new do-gooder mission: helping the underdog Democratic Party to flourish in the predominantly Republican state of Wisconsin. She was especially talented at creating campaign literature, and her catchy slogans helped draw attention to Democratic candidates and issues. Before long she was appointed head of Eau Claire's Democratic Party speakers bureau, responsible for attracting important lecturers like Hubert Humphrey, then a U.S. senator from Minnesota. But when she ran in 1953 for the Democratic county chairman position—against the head of the workers' union at Presto—the election was transformed into a mythic contest between "the working man" and the executive's wife, or the "society candidate," as she was called.

She lost the race, but Eppie immediately demanded another vote, her public statement making headlines in the local paper: "Election Rigged, Packed, and Stacked—A Phony." She won the second election by a three-to-one margin. However, the friction created during the two controversial elections resulted in serious union problems for the Presto company, where eventually more than 1,000 laborers were let go. Jules chose to leave Presto soon after, and the Lederers decided to move to their favorite city, Chicago. As a result, just six months after her election victory, Eppie resigned as county Democratic chairman. When the Lederers left Eau Claire in late 1954 the local paper ran an editorial warning Chicago to "watch out for Eppie Lederer—she'll make her mark on the city."

The career choices Eppie had made in Eau Claire were extraordinary ones at the time because they were so unconventional. During the 1950s, few women sought careers outside marriage and motherhood unless economic circumstances necessitated working outside the home. Eppie Lederer, however, wanted to be something more than a wife and mother, and she intended to "do good" in a very big way.

During the summer of 1954, the Lederers moved

Eppie had established herself as a political presence in Eau Claire, Wisconsin, and had even won the race for Democratic county chairperson when Jules, whose position at Presto was affected by the controversial election, decided to leave his company. The couple moved to Chicago, Illinois, into a luxury apartment on the city's Lake Shore Drive, shown here.

into a three-bedroom apartment on Chicago's Lake Shore Drive and into a world of uniformed doormen, screeching taxis, and the hubbub of urban living. Jules became president of Autopoint Corporation, an advertising firm dealing mainly in ballpoint pens. Eppie spent a great deal of time redesigning their 40th-floor lakeview home, but before long she grew bored with housekeeping. She decided to take a shot at becoming the Democratic national committeewoman for Illinois.

Eppie quickly realized that the politics of Chicago was very different from that of Eau Claire. In Chicago, it was a cutthroat, dangerous, big-city game. One person advised her to abandon politics and take up golf instead, since there were hundreds of Chicago women who were far more qualified to be a committeewoman.

At home Eppie now had a staff that included a full-time cook/housekeeper, who assisted whenever Eppie entertained Jules's business associates. With all the help, Mrs. Lederer found herself with plenty of time on her hands. She felt restless, and she told Popo, "I want to use my brain and do something different." Eppie knew that she did not want merely to get involved in volunteer efforts such as charity work and fund-raising. "I had a lot of energy and knew it was time to do something else," Eppie recalls. "I wanted to serve, to do something for someone else."

"Mother knew she had a calling," Margo states in her book, *Eppie*. "She just didn't know what it was." Then, one morning in August 1955, Eppie found herself reading and rereading the lovelorn column, called "Your Problems," in the *Chicago Sun-Times*. And she suddenly realized exactly what she wanted to do: she would assist the lovelorn columnist! Eppie immediately phoned Wilbur Munnecke, a *Sun-Times* executive whom she had befriended years before. Might the columnist Ann Landers need help answering her mail?

"Funny you should ask," Munnecke responded. "It is odd that you are calling me now. Ruth Crowley, our Ann Landers, died suddenly last week." The newspaper was, in fact, seeking a replacement for Crowley. When Eppie suggested that she could be the new Ann Landers, Munnecke laughed out loud. Crowley had been a journalist and a nurse. Her column was syndicated in more than two dozen newspapers. Eppie Lederer was a housewife without a college degree, and more than 25 other women, many of whom were experienced journalists, had applied for the position.

Ruth Crowley's photograph had always accompanied her popular column, written under the pen name Ann Landers, and the editors were hoping to keep the death and "rebirth" of Ann Landers a secret. For this reason, the editors of the *Sun-Times* were specifically looking for a woman who resembled the dark-haired woman, who had been in her late thirties when the photograph was taken. Physically at least, Eppie was perfect for the position. Most important, however, was the fact that she wanted the job very badly.

Eppie hurried over to the offices of the *Sun-Times* to pick up the package of materials being given to applicants. She recalls meeting Larry Fanning, an editor who was temporarily writing the column. He "stared in disbelief" when the housewife of 16 years candidly admitted her complete lack of credentials. "You might as well try," Fanning told the determined Eppie. "You have nothing to lose."

On her way home from the *Sun-Times*, Eppie realized that she would need a typewriter, so she rented an IBM. "To buy one would be presumptuous," she thought at the time.

Eppie Lederer had never held a paying job and had just had her very first look at the inside of a newspaper office. But she had plenty of confidence in her own judgment, her old-fashioned common sense, and her ideas of what was right and wrong. She also possessed an amazing store of energy, and she had made a number of important connections with her outgoing personality and former political career.

The packet of materials for applicants for the "Your Problems" column consisted of a stack of hypothetical readers' problems. Each applicant received an identical set of letters, and the editors who judged the submissions did not know the identities of any of the competitors. Eppie took three weeks to develop 40 sample columns, which she turned in under the byline "XYZ."

Ruth Crowley had written "Your Problems" using the pseudonym *Ann Landers* for 13 years. The column had a snappy tone and provided down-to-earth advice. Eppie Lederer wrote—and spoke—in this very style. And she knew how to back up her own intuitive answers to readers' problems with input from professionals with experience and credibility. For example, to answer a question about who owned the walnuts that fell from a woman's tree into her neighbor's yard, Eppie called on U.S. Supreme Court justice William O.

Under the tutelage of managing editor Larry Fanning of the Chicago Sun-Times, *Eppie became a skillful advice columnist. Less than a year after she began her new career, her column "Your Problems" was syndicated in 300 newspapers throughout the United States.*

Douglas. He told her that the neighbor could legally keep the nuts herself but she could not sell them. Eppie also sought input from other professionals with impressive credentials, including her old friend Dr. Robert Stolar, whom she turned to for advice on a question about psychosomatic (emotionally induced) hives.

A few days after submitting her carefully researched sample columns, Eppie received a call from Marshall Field, the publisher of the *Sun-Times*. "Good morning, Ann Landers," he greeted the new columnist. "Of course I was thrilled . . . and still am pinching myself," Eppie recalled of the day she was hired by the *Sun-Times* to pen the four-days-a-week column. Her weekly salary was $87. "The manner in which the column fell into my lap is enough to make a person believe in Santa Claus," she stated humbly.

In reality, Eppie had earned her new byline, beating out more experienced writers because she was a highly innovative researcher with an appealingly clever writing style. Before she even got the job, Eppie Lederer *was* Ann Landers.

The new Ann Landers arrived at the *Sun-Times* newsroom for her first day of work in October 1955 to find her desk buried under thousands of unopened letters. She had no secretary, no telephone, and no private office. "The copy boy greeted me with, 'So, you're the new Ann Landers. Well, here's your mail.' He then dumped about 5,000 letters on my desk. I didn't know whether to laugh or cry," she remembered.

The executives at the *Sun-Times* were not sure whether the housewife from Sioux City would be able to handle the demands of the job, so they kept her identity a secret and refrained from giving her a contract for the first six months she worked for them. "You'll never last," one of them informed her.

Larry Fanning, however, took the new writer under his wing and quickly taught Eppie how to shape her column, balancing human interest stories with professional advice and a touch of humor. "He called everybody 'baby,'" Eppie recalled years later in an interview published in *Psychology Today*. "He said, 'Baby, some of these letters are going to kill you, but you've got to remember that what they are telling you is happening to them, not you. You have to learn how to separate yourself from those readers.'"

Fanning not only served as Eppie's dedicated editor but he also became a mentor and friend. Together they weathered Eppie's trial period at the *Sun-Times* as she evolved into a skilled advice columnist. In less than a year, Ann Landers and "Your Problems" had become so popular that its syndication expanded to more than 300 newspapers. "It caught on like wildfire," Eppie recounts. "I had no competition. There was nobody else around—I mean nobody."

Well, *almost* nobody.

Popo Phillips, better known as Abigail Van Buren, in the 1960s. Even as the wealthy new wife of an executive, Popo followed the example of her parents and stayed involved in numerous charitable organizations. "I learned to listen," she said of one of her volunteer stints as a Gray Lady in an Eau Claire hospital.

4

FROM "POPO" TO ABIGAIL VAN BUREN

Dear Abby: Our daughter-in-law was married in January. Five months later she had a nine-pound baby girl. She said the baby was premature. Tell me, can a baby this big be that early?
—Wondering

Dear Wondering: The baby was on time. The wedding was late. Forget about it.

●   ●   ●

Dear Abby: What is the cure for a man who has been married for 33 years and still can't stay away from other women?
—His Wife

Dear Wife: Rigor mortis.

●   ●   ●

Dear Abby: Socrates was a very smart man. They poisoned him. Please be careful.

—Love, Allen

Popo relaxes poolside with her family in 1958, two years after transforming herself into advice columnist Abigail Van Buren. From left to right are son Eddie, husband Mort, Popo, and daughter Jeannie.

Before she became Mrs. Morton Phillips, Popo had never lived outside her parents' home. She stayed in touch with A. B. and Becky by writing to them from her new home in an upscale area of Minneapolis. "I got tremendous satisfaction by writing a letter to my parents every day that they lived. And I didn't miss a day," Popo has stated.

She also wrote many letters to Eppie, sharing with her the details of her new role as the wife of a rich executive. Later Popo admitted, "When I got married at twenty-one it never entered my head to be anything but a wife. I played golf and bridge and had lunch with the girls. I was bored out of my gourd."

A daughter, Etta Jean (Jeannie), was born in 1942, and a son, Edward Jay (Eddie), arrived three years later.

When Eddie was a few months old, the Phillips family moved to Eau Claire, where Mort became executive vice president of National Presto Industries. Popo found a large fieldstone house in a well-to-do neighborhood and hired a full-time governess and live-in couple who cooked and kept house.

For Popo, married life was blissful. She was crazy about Mort and happy with their lavish lifestyle. Her ever-expanding shoe collection, which consisted primarily of stiletto-heeled pumps, filled the floor-to-ceiling shelves of a specially built closet. Popo favored Paris fashions, loved vacationing in Palm Springs, Florida, and soon developed an affinity for celebrities in the entertainment world. Her friends included the famous actress Jane Russell, singer and talk-show host Dinah Shore, and *Lassie* star June Allyson. Popo even managed to earn a small film role in the 1951 motion picture *At War with the Army*, during which she befriended costars Jerry Lewis and Dean Martin.

Home and family were Popo's priority, however, and she rose early each morning to see her family off to work and school. She loved to bake for them: according to her niece Margo, her aunt was indeed "a wonderful baker and her desserts had more than a casual acquaintance with chocolate and whipped cream." Popo also loved monkeys—stuffed, ceramic, and wooden, even paintings of monkeys—and acquired a pair of live monkeys she named David and Bathsheba. The monkeys lived in a cage behind the Phillipses' house, but they escaped a little too frequently to climb the neighbors' trees. Eventually, the monkeys were sent to a zoo. "They're just impossible to train," Popo explained afterward.

Popo also spent a great deal of time doing volunteer work, for which she seemed to have unbounded energy. Like her sister, she worked as a Gray Lady at the Luther Hospital in Eau Claire, and she became active in a number of other charitable organizations in town. "In Eau

After the Phillipses settled in San Francisco in 1955, Popo began to feel restless. With her children in private schools and plenty of hired help for household chores, she longed for an outlet for her energy. She found it by helping Eppie with her new advice column.

Claire, I learned how many people are hurting," Popo explained years later. "I learned to listen."

Popo had just settled the Phillips family into their newest home—a spacious ranch house with a swimming pool, located in a ritzy suburb of San Francisco called Hillsborough—when Eppie became the new Ann Landers. Eppie immediately shared her excitement and anxiety over the new job with her twin. By this time, Jeannie and Eddie attended private schools and Mort was busy as the president of the family-owned liquor distributorship, M. Sellers and Company. "I took stock of myself," Popo recalls of this time. "I was a 37-year-old housewife with two teenagers, plenty of help in the house, and time on my hands. I was bursting with energy."

Her energy found an outlet in October 1955, when she began assisting her twin in writing the "Ann Landers" column. "For the first few months Eppie sent me batches of letters from readers and I'd shoot back my suggested replies. Many were used, and I became fascinated with the opportunity to do something creative, entertaining, and helpful. I was ecstatically happy and having a ball!" Popo remembers in *The Best of Dear Abby*.

"Then, suddenly," she says, "the ball was over."

When the *Sun-Times* discovered the sisters' collaboration, its editors expressed harsh disapproval. They forbade Eppie from sending any readers' letters out of the newspaper office. Popo was crushed. But when she looked over a pile of letters she was about to return to Eppie, Popo realized that she, too, could write an advice column of her own.

"I was sure I could," Popo recounts. "I've always been a compulsive letter writer." For years she also had been composing clever poems, sending them to friends with the pseudonym "Edgar Allan Popo," a play on the name of the famous 19th-century author Edgar Allan Poe. Popo was confident about her ability to listen and to help others. After all, she reasoned, she had been doing so for more than 15 years in her volunteer work. And she felt buoyed by the knowledge that she had been providing input to Ann Landers, who was growing more and more popular with the publication of each sassy column.

Popo's first attempt to obtain a columnist position was a failure. When she approached the editor of a small daily paper only a few minutes from her home, she was abruptly turned down, even after she offered to write the column for free. Discouraged but not dissuaded, Popo began to think about the Molly Mayfield lovelorn column that she read every morning in the *San Francisco Chronicle*. "The answers weren't helpful," she claims. "They lacked imagination. I could always come up with a better solution."

In early January 1956, Popo once again read over

the Molly Mayfield column. "I'll never forget that day," she said many years later. "A woman had written into the paper with genuine despair. She had gone from man to man seeking real love, and that columnist had accused her of learning her morals in an alley. I was furious." Impulsively, Popo telephoned the newspaper and asked to speak to the feature editor, Stanleigh "Auk" Arnold. Identifying herself as a "Hillsborough housewife" with an "interesting proposition," Popo blurted out, "It's about that advice column you're running. It's pretty grim."

"And I suppose *you* can write a better one," the editor barked back. "Fall in line. A lot of people tell me that."

"Then maybe it's time you listened," Popo countered.

"Well, if you're ever in the neighborhood, come in and see me," Arnold replied, curtly ending the conversation.

The next morning, Popo had her chauffeur drive her to the *Chronicle* where, dressed in a Dior dress and a leopard-skin coat, she met with the 6' 5" Auk Arnold. The amused editor failed to inform his flashy little visitor that he was, in fact, hunting for a replacement for Molly Mayfield. The Mayfield column was only a temporary one that filled a slot left by the "Ann Landers" column—which the *Chronicle* had lost to its rival, the *San Francisco Call-Bulletin*. "I was charged with finding somebody to replace the Ann Landers column," Arnold stated years later. "We tried several writers but they just didn't have the zip of Landers."

When Popo recounted for him her "experience" as a Morningside College student columnist and charity volunteer, she recalls that Arnold was "visibly underwhelmed." Nevertheless, he handed Popo a stack of unanswered letters Mayfield had received the previous week, and he sent her home to answer them.

Undaunted, Popo zipped over to her husband's office a few blocks away, where she borrowed a typewriter "and whacked out my answers. They were mostly flip, saucy one-liners. Two hours later I was back at the

Attired in fur, jewels, and a glittering gown, Popo attends a formal function as Abigail Van Buren. Popo's marriage to Mort Phillips allowed her to lead a life of leisure and indulge in lavish shopping sprees and expensive vacations. But when the feature editor of the San Francisco Chronicle *dared her to improve on the newspaper's advice column, Popo accepted the difficult challenge with enthusiasm.*

Chronicle rattling Auk Arnold's cage." Less than an hour later, when Popo arrived home again, her phone was ringing: it was Arnold, requesting that she return to the *Chronicle*'s offices. "There was not a question that she was exactly what we were looking for," Arnold remembers. "I went in immediately to the managing editor and publisher and said, 'I think we have what we want.'"

The pay was 20 dollars per column, which was fine with Popo, who would have written the column for free. But she was adamant about selecting an appropriate pen name and claiming legal ownership of the pseudonym—and thereby the columns—herself. Mort Phillips counseled his wife to be sure that she retained these rights. It turned out to be an extremely fortuitous piece of business advice.

"The name, of course, was Abigail Van Buren," Popo says. "I took the 'Abigail' from the Old Testament, for Abigail was a prophetess in the Book of Samuel, and it was said of her, 'Blessed art thou, and blessed is thy advice, O Abigail.' For my last name I chose 'Van Buren' from our eighth president Martin Van Buren, because I liked the aristocratic, old-family ring," she states in *The Best of Dear Abby*. The column was named "Dear Abby" because Popo believed this sounded inviting, like someone to whom she herself would feel comfortable writing.

Unlike Eppie, who engaged in a scrupulous editing process with her editor, Abby received little input from Auk Arnold, who felt that "the copy spoke for itself." On January 9, 1956, "Dear Abby" made its debut in the *San Francisco Chronicle*. Abby immediately began to receive what she referred to as a "cascade" of readers' responses. Within two weeks, she had to hire a secretary to help her handle the onslaught of mail.

As soon as her deal with the *Chronicle* was settled, Popo telephoned Eppie to tell her the good news. Eppie was less than thrilled, however, to learn that she would now share her newly formed solo identity as an advice columnist with her twin. "When Popo told Mother about the *Chronicle*, the announcement was received with frosty interest," recalls Margo in her biography of Eppie. "Popo became the imitator. Maybe it was their destiny to remain two. Once again the Friedman twins were a sister act."

"She seemed disturbed," Popo admitted to *LIFE* magazine in 1958 when asked how Eppie received the news that her twin had created "Dear Abby." "I had been so happy over her success that I assumed she would be happy for me. But there was a long silence, and finally she said, 'I guess it's all right if you don't get syndicated.'"

But then the *New York Mirror* picked up "Dear Abby" in late January 1956. Since the tabloid boasted one of the nation's largest circulations, it became clear that the column was about to acquire enormous prestige and a huge national readership. So Popo signed a 10-year contract with McNaught Syndicate, a large organization that would sell her column to newspapers all over the country. By the end of its first year, "Dear Abby" was syndicated in more than 80 papers. *Time* magazine hailed Popo's column as being "slicker, quicker, and flipper than her twin sister's."

Popo claims that she would have been "perfectly content to write exclusively for the *Chronicle*, and had I not been offered the *New York Mirror*, the thought of syndication would never have crossed my mind." But she also admits that she knew her sister felt betrayed. Popo also said that she was beginning to feel "an unmistakably cool breeze from the windy city of Chicago," where her sister lived.

In a rare photograph, all four Friedman sisters—Dorothy (Mrs. Morey Rubin), Eppie (Ann Landers), Popo (Abigail Van Buren), and Helen (Mrs. David Brodkey)—pose during the wedding reception of a cousin in 1983. Dorothy and Helen were both married by the time the twins were in high school, so they felt little jealousy over the pampering their younger sisters received. Between the twins themselves, however, friendly competition developed into an intense professional rivalry after they earned fame as advice columnists.

5

THE FEUD

On July 2, 1964, the following unusually personal "Dear Abby" column appeared in newspapers across the country:

Dear Mort:

Today is a very special day for me. It's my twenty-fifth wedding anniversary, and I have this to say: I had a mother and father who really loved each other, so I know what love is.

I have worked hard to see two teen-agers safely through their traumatic teens, so I know what satisfaction is.

I have prayed. And my prayers have been answered, so I know what faith is.

I have had by my side the kindest, gentlest, most considerate human being I've ever known, so I know what happiness is.

And because I've known all these things . . . I know what wealth is. I love you.

—Abby

Five years later, on July 2, 1969, Ann Landers printed the following, one of her few personal columns:

When Ann Landers and Abigail Van Buren launched their advice columns in the mid-1950s, America's social climate was decidedly conservative.

Dear Readers: This may be just another day to you, but it is a very special day in my life. Thirty years ago, on a sweltering Sunday afternoon in Sioux City, Iowa, Jules Lederer slipped a plain gold band on my finger, and I became his wife. . . .

A good marriage, it is said, is made in heaven. This might be true, but the maintenance work must be done right down here. A successful marriage is not a gift, it is an achievement. No real marriage can exist without differences in opinion and the ensuing battles. But battles can be healthy. They bring to marriage the vital principle of equal partnership. If there is a secret to making mar-

riage work, it is "Never go to bed mad.". . .

*Being Ann Landers' husband could pose a terrible prob-
lem, but Jules has met the challenge with dignity and
incredible good humor. My husband is my best friend, and
I am his. I consider it a privilege to be the wife of this beautiful guy, who took on the world with a ninth-grade education and a hole in his sock.*

●   ●   ●

When Eppie Lederer churned out her very first
"Ann Landers" column for the *Chicago Sun-Times* on
October 16, 1955, it cost only three cents to mail a letter. The political mood of the country was conservative, and network television, born in 1947, was still
new to most Americans. Ann Landers's breezy advice
about acceptable standards of behavior, crackling with
puns, one-liners and trademark expressions, was perfectly suited to the times.

In her first column, Ann responded to a fan of auto
racing who had fallen for a married woman in spite of
his own 10-year marriage and two sons: "Time wounds
all heels—and you'll get yours. . . . The way you're
headed, you will get exactly what you deserve." To a
junior high school girl who wanted to date an army
man against her mother's wishes, Ann warned, "Uncle
Sam needs men—you don't. Listen to your mother; she
is right. And about that boyfriend—his brains must be
AWOL." She advised a pregnant wife to give her cheat-
ing husband another chance: "Try to persuade him to
go with you to a marriage counselor." And to "Steady
Reader" who wondered why her busy delivery-man
beau only visited once a day when he brought food to
her home, Ann suggested that the "back-door Romeo"
was probably married and had best be forgotten.

Readers enjoyed Ann Landers's sentimentality and
sense of humor, and many of them felt comfortable
enough to tell her off. An early reader who felt that

Ann's advice on teen dating was outmoded sniped, "Why don't YOU wake up and smell the coffee?" Ann fostered this sense of intimacy with her expressions of genuine concern for individual readers, whom she comforted with such nurturing comments as, "I'm betting on you" or "Good luck, honey."

Letters to Ann came from doctors, clergymen, and politicians, as well as hairdressers, truckers, school-teachers, and cashiers. Teenagers often wrote to complain or inquire about rules, schools, and the opposite sex. After less than five years in print, Eppie's "Ann Landers" column boasted a readership of 35 million.

In the meantime, "Dear Abby" had also become a big hit with readers. Rapidly scooped up by newspapers across the country, the column was heralded as "a phenomenon in modern journalism" and Abigail Van Buren as "the fastest rising star in the business." Abby's speedy success was due in large part to her flippant style, which was a bit naughty for the morally conservative 1950s and was often regarded as being outright racy.

During the first month of publication, for example, a woman whose fiancé had run off to Alaska wondered how she should tell him that she was pregnant. "In English, and fast," Abby responded. When a 24-year-old wrote that his landlady had asked him to marry her, Abby warned, "You need a 38-year-old widow with five kids like a moose needs a hat rack."

Small-city newspapers were wary of running "Dear Abby" at first, afraid that her brash humor might offend middle-American sensibilities. But the column gained readers at an unprecedented pace, and its popularity skyrocketed.

The cool breeze that Popo once said she felt coming from Chicago quickly turned icy.

"We started our columns within a few weeks of each other," bragged Popo, "but I became more quickly and more broadly syndicated before [Eppie]." Also, whereas Eppie remained an employee of her newspaper, which

held sole ownership of the *Ann Landers* title and the "Your Problems" column, Popo had had the foresight to retain all rights to "Dear Abby." This meant that Popo had the legal right to sign on with interested newspapers, publish books, and appear in public as Abigail Van Buren at her own discretion—and she could receive direct payment for her work as Dear Abby. Eppie, on the other hand, received a salary from the *Sun-Times*, whose editors determined where the column—and Ann Landers herself—appeared. As a result, while Popo wielded total control over her column and earned a large share of the profits from "Dear Abby," Eppie did not gain ownership of the *Ann Landers* name for another 10 years. She also had to wait more than 30 years before her contract allowed her the kind of control her sister enjoyed from the start.

Eppie became the first of the twins to appear on television when she was invited to be a "mystery guest" on the game show What's My Line? *In each episode of the program, a panel of celebrities (shown here with host John Daly, far right) tried to guess the occupations of contestants by asking them questions that required "yes" or "no" answers only. During one segment of each show, the panelists were blindfolded while they questioned the mystery guest.*

Despite the limitations imposed on her by her contract, Eppie was the first of the twins to appear on television. Six months after she began writing her column, she was allowed to make public appearances as Ann Landers. Eppie readily accepted when the popular game show *What's My Line?* asked her to be a guest. The *Sun-Times* reluctantly gave permission for her to appear on the program, and millions of TV viewers learned that Eppie Friedman Lederer from Sioux City, Iowa, was actually the saucy new advice columnist headquartered in Chicago.

Two years later, Popo made *her* television debut. "When Edward R. Murrow, the famous radio-television commentator, asked if he could televise me and my family from our home in Hillsborough on *Person to Person*, I felt that I had really arrived," Popo recalled. The celebrity-studded show included visits with the notorious duke and duchess of Windsor as well as famed Hollywood icon Elizabeth Taylor, so when Dear Abby was introduced, millions of viewers were already tuned in.

By the time "Dear Abby" began running in the twins' hometown newspaper, the *Sioux City Journal*, the intense professional rivalry between the two was public knowledge. If Ann Landers told the press that she received two thousand letters a week, Abigail Van Buren would announce that she heard from *seven* thousand readers. When Popo stated that a dozen new papers had signed up to run "Dear Abby," Eppie would roll off an even longer list of new subscribers to the Ann Landers column.

Since negative publicity is often regarded as better than no publicity at all, the sisters' newspaper syndicates were content to let the rather petty public rivalry between them fester. In addition, many cities had at least two newspapers competing for the same readers. Often, one would purchase "Dear Abby" while the other ran "Your Problems." So the heated competition between

Two years after Eppie's TV debut, Popo appeared as Abigail Van Buren on Person to Person, *a prime-time interview show hosted by the legendary Edward R. Murrow. Technological advances allowed Murrow to interview his guests in their homes while he remained in CBS-TV's New York studio, shown here in 1956.*

the twins was almost encouraged by the business in which they were involved.

In April 1958, *LIFE* magazine illustrated just how strained the advice sisters' relationship had become. A journalist and a photographer from the magazine documented the private lives and thoughts of Ann Landers and Abigail Van Buren by camping out for several days in each sister's home. Not surprisingly, Eppie and Popo were no longer speaking to one another by that time, but they carped at each other in print and their words were heart-piercingly sharp.

Popo traced Eppie's case of sibling rivalry back to their childhood. "I understand why she's disturbed," Popo confided to the *LIFE* reporter. "She wanted to be the first violin in the school orchestra, but I was. She swore she'd marry a millionaire, but I did. I'm not trying to be the champion. It's just like playing poker. If you don't have to win, you get the cards, and she's always just had to win."

In her interview Eppie responded by snapping, "That's her fantasy. She's just like a kid who beats a dog until somebody looks, and then starts petting it."

About their years together in Wisconsin, Popo insinuated that her husband had hired Eppie's husband as a favor to *her*, stating, "I didn't want a mink coat if she couldn't have one, too. Of course, in Eau Claire she was always known as Popo's sister."

Eppie replied indignantly, "We went to Eau Claire because [Jules] was the best salesman Presto ever had and because Mort needed somebody solid beside him." She defended her husband as well, arguing, "She's as wrong as when she says I wanted to marry a millionaire. I didn't have to. She's the one who needs the assurance of money." Eppie asked the *LIFE* reporter, "How long am I going to have her hanging over me?"

Abby in turn wanted to know, "When is she going to stop behaving like this?"

In response to the twins' anguished questions, *LIFE* provided the following Ann- and Abby-like answers:

Dear Ann: Forever.
Dear Abby: Never.

LIFE magazine titled the resulting piece "Twin Lovelorn Advisors Torn Asunder by Success." The article accused the two columnists of "using U.S. journalism as a personal battlefield and its hundreds of newspapers as personal artillery in what must be the most feverish female feud since Elizabeth sent Mary Queen of Scots to the chopping block."

The rush of publicity that followed *LIFE*'s cover story boosted the popularity of both sisters' columns. Ironically, increasing numbers of readers sought the advice of two columnists who seemed incapable of straightening out their own relationship with one another.

In the late 1950s Ann Landers's seventh-floor office at the *Chicago Sun-Times* had pink walls, pink carpeting, and pink furniture. Three secretaries helped handle her mail, organized her hectic public speaking schedule, and answered her phones. Although Eppie went into the office every day, she did all of her writing at home. "I work ten and twelve hours a day—six days a week," she admitted. Her 700-word column appeared daily in more than 100 papers.

Abby worked at home, too, although she sat at the electric typewriter in her bedroom for only four hours a day. She compiled a best-selling book of her columns, which she titled *Dear Abby*. Both sisters also wrote pamphlets on a variety of subjects ranging from the dangers of teen alcohol use to wedding etiquette. The pamphlets were advertised at the end of each column.

Popo steadfastly claims that she and her sister never stopped speaking to one another, and Eppie admitted that "if anyone had written to me with [a similar] problem, I would have said, 'Forgive and forget.'" Nevertheless, the public feud and private silence between the twins dragged on for years. The annual double birthday and wedding anniversary celebration was canceled, of course, and the two couples toasted their happiness separately each July for nearly a decade. For most of that time, their family members viewed the bitter battle between the sisters as a temporary rift between "squabbling girls." Nevertheless, Jules Lederer remarked during this difficult time, "Blood is thicker than water and it boils faster, too." And Mort Phillips half-joked, "If these are twin sisters, I'll take cobras."

Protesters in London, England, campaign for equal rights for gay men and women in this 1974 photo. Though Ann Landers is considered relatively conservative in her moral views, she was among the first columnists in America to discuss openly the subject of homosexuality.

6

CHANGING TIMES

*D*ear Ann Landers: Last night, I had sex with 4,097 people. Impossible, you say? You're wrong.

I'm a divorced woman who has had a faithful lover for quite some time. Last night, I had too much to drink, and like a crazy fool, I had sex with a man I had seen several times at our tennis club. He admitted having sex with eight "perfectly respectable" female partners over the last year.

I worked a chart backward the same as in our tennis seeding. I took those eight women and assumed that they also had slept with eight men each, and each of those eight men had had sex with eight women, etc.

By using simple arithmetic progression, after only three series, I realized that I had been exposed somewhere along the line to 4,096 persons, plus one.

How can I assume that there was no one in that family tree who was not an AIDS carrier, if only through a blood transfusion. . . .
—Scared

Dear Scared: You have focused on the aspect of AIDS that makes it such a terrifying disease. Add to the nightmare this horror: A person

Abigail Van Buren (Popo Phillips), shown here in a photo that ran for years alongside her daily column. During the turbulent 1960s and early 1970s, Abby strove to keep up with the times by asking her children, Eddie and Jeannie, for their opinions on controversial topics.

can have the AIDS virus without knowing it and infect a partner.

More and more, it appears that the only way to ensure staying healthy is abstinence or a monogamous relationship with someone who is perfectly safe.

●   ●   ●

Dear Ann Landers: The way the homosexuals are taking over the country, a straight person is considered an oddity. . . . And now, I see there's a church out in Hollywood (natch) that has a fairy pastor and a congregation composed of nearly 300 fags and lesbians. . . . This clergy-

man recently announced that he will "marry" homosex-
ual couples.

—*Resident of the World's Largest*
Open-Air Lunatic Asylum—Los Angeles

*Dear Los Angeles: If homosexuals want to pray as a
group, it's all right with me. I'm more concerned about
the violent people in our society.*

●   ●   ●

*Dear Abby: Another advice columnist keeps insisting
that homosexuals are "sick." She says, and I quote: "Thousands of homosexuals have written asking me where they
can get 'straightened out,' so they must consider themselves
sick—or they wouldn't be asking for help. Occasionally I
hear from homosexuals who are at peace with themselves,
but they are few and far between. I believe the majority of
homosexuals would be straight if they were really free to
choose." What do you say, Dear Abby?*

—*L.A. Times Reader*

*Dear Reader: I say if a heterosexual had been raised to
believe that his preference for the opposite sex was "sick,"
twisted, abominable, sinful, and a disgrace to his family, he
would ask for help on how to "straighten himself out," too.*

*Homosexuality is a problem because an unenlightened
society has made it a problem, but I have received letters
by the thousands (not just "occasionally") from gay people
telling me that they wouldn't be straight if they had a
choice. All they ask is to be allowed to love in their own
way without facing the charge that they are "sick and
twisted."*

I say, love and let love.

●   ●   ●

Ann Landers has told her readers, "The changes I

have seen would twirl your turban." Certainly, the social upheaval and shifting moral values of the 1960s gave Eppie Lederer pause. And there she was, right in the thick of it, combing through tall stacks of letters every day on topics, such as homosexuality, that were once regarded as taboo in mixed company and banned from print.

As Dear Abby, Popo too sifted through readers' queries on sensitive subjects to which her conservative upbringing had failed to expose her. Among the more naive missives about problems with acne, prom dates, nosy neighbors, and lazy spouses, an increasing number of letters concerned more serious topics, clearly illustrating that a tidal change in society's mores was taking place.

As early as her first year in print, Ann Landers tackled the very controversial issue of sexual orientation. She published a letter from a young man who wondered how he might convince his parents to accept his same-sex romantic partner. At that time, homosexuality was almost never discussed in public. Not surprisingly, one Michigan newspaper refused to print the column. Instead, the publisher of the paper in the small town of St. Joseph ran a front-page notice explaining that the "Ann Landers" column would not appear that day due to content unfit for family reading.

Years later, Landers described the incident to a journalist from the *New Yorker:* "I called the publisher up and said, 'This is a human problem, and that is what I do.' He said, 'I'm not going to print it.' I said, 'Fine. Then everyone in St. Joe is going to buy the *Detroit Free Press* to see what you won't print.' I called the *Free Press* and told them to get ready for a lot of extra sales because I know human nature. 'They're going to buy the other paper to find out what it is, this 'isn't fit for family reading [business],' I said. Well, that was the last time I had to do something like that. From then on, boy, that St. Joe paper printed every damn word I

wrote." In the 1960s, the middle-class values of the previous decade were being challenged, and long-established social roles were undergoing reconstruction. Parents and children, men and women, husbands and wives were no longer clearly defined by their "assigned" duties and privileges. Ann Landers's readers reflected that confusion. Eppie Lederer was careful to uphold time-honored principles while introducing commentary on the changes she felt that her readers were struggling to absorb.

Early on, Ann Landers dared to acknowledge the reality that some teens were sexually active. This acknowledgment made her opinions appear very advanced for the time. "Old-fashioned philosophy is fine, Dad, but don't overlook old-fashioned chemistry," she advised one concerned father of teens. She was among the first to use the phrase that a woman's body is her own. But her printed views did not always keep up with the accelerating pace of social changes, and she lagged behind in some aspects. For example, Ann Landers continued to emphasize the importance of pleasing one's husband in a marriage. She frowned upon marked age differences between marriage partners, and she discouraged interfaith relationships. Until 1965, she also shied away from using the word "sex" in her column to describe intercourse.

Ann Landers's column was so popular that one could almost track societal trends by examining the way she used language. In 1962, for example, she used the term "make out" in her column for the first time. Two years later, she used the word "menopause" in place of gentle euphemisms such as "that time of life." In 1965 Ann boldly employed the terms "syphilis" and "breast," words that were once considered too explicit to print in a newspaper column. A young woman in her column admitted to having an abortion in 1966. Not until the 1970s, however, were controversial terms like "incest," "rape," and "gays" and subjects like street drugs mentioned by name in the "Ann Landers" column.

Abby also altered her language and her advice during the turbulent 1960s. On the more controversial topics of the era, Popo consulted her own children, Jeannie and Eddie, who espoused the liberal beliefs of most people of their generation. Long talks with her teens and their friends often prompted Popo to make significant changes in Abby's professional counsel. "I've gone through a gradual process of loosening my views as my children became adults, and they and their

Eppie's involvement in Eau Claire politics allowed her to forge friendships with powerful political figures like Senator Hubert H. Humphrey, shown here in 1977. Popo, meanwhile, was boosting her own reputation as Abigail Van Buren by publishing advice books and earning citations such as the Los Angeles Helping Hand "Mother of the Year" award.

friends taught me that maybe I was a little out of step," Popo confessed.

In the radically altered world of American life, critics became increasingly unappreciative of the pop psychology and liberal politics offered by Dear Abby and Ann Landers. But the two columnists continued to state their positions on social issues, striving to stay up-to-date on the changing culture of America.

When Eppie first took over the "Ann Landers" column, she usually consulted her good friend Dr. Robert

Stolar whenever she felt the need for a second opinion. But as the "Ann Landers" column began to receive national recognition, Eppie turned more often to professional specialists and top authorities across the country. As Ann Landers, Eppie was not afraid to admit her errors and was openly willing to revise her positions when challenged by persuasive readers.

On frequent trips to Washington, D.C., she also fostered friendships with powerful political figures such as Senator Hubert Humphrey, her friend from her involvement in Eau Claire politics. Eppie networked with other important men, including Lyndon Johnson, who became president of the United States in 1963 after the assassination of President John F. Kennedy. Eppie also befriended the president of the University of Notre Dame, Father Theodore Hesburgh, who was once labeled "the most powerful priest in America" by *Time* magazine.

To demonstrate her concern over political issues of national and international importance, Eppie also traveled to the Soviet Union in 1959. Her three-week tour resulted in a series of 12 articles, which ran in nearly 100 U.S. newspapers. In the articles, Eppie shared her discovery that "the problems of people are the same the world over. . . . Iran is worried about Irena's supervision at the factory. . . . Trina is concerned about Alexander's excessive drinking. . . . Elina has a lecherous boss. . . . [and] Igor hates his mother-in-law." Her sensitive and humane coverage of the Russian people during a time when the United States was engaged in a "cold war" with the Soviet Union established Ann Landers as a contemporary figure with valuable opinions on world politics.

In 1961, Ann Landers visited a leper colony in Nassau, Bahamas, with Dr. Stolar, and she strongly encouraged her readers to replace fear of this dreadful disease with compassion for those who suffered from it. In 1967, she completed a grueling 10-day tour of hospi-

tals throughout Vietnam. By this time a certified celebrity, Ann Landers was welcomed by the wounded and homesick American soldiers who were stationed there during the Vietnam War. One army officer informed the press, "Most celebrities who come here walk through a couple of wards, get their pictures taken, and leave. This woman has visited every single patient. It's almost eleven at night and I know she's been on her feet since this morning. Where in the world does that little woman get her energy?"

Eppie's enthusiasm continued even after she returned to the United States: she brought back 300 phone numbers for the families of the soldiers she had befriended overseas, and in the next few weeks she called every one of them.

Despite the critics who labeled Abigail Van Buren and Ann Landers as out of step with America's changing social values during the 1960s, both columnists continued to receive mountains of mail from readers seeking advice and reassurance.

Eppie was against American involvement in the Vietnam War at a time when vocal opposition was still limited to a minority of students and some members of the clergy. Nevertheless, she visited the soldiers stationed in Vietnam and did not publicly criticize U.S. engagement in the war until much later, when national opinion polls showed that the majority of Americans felt the same way she did. As Ann Landers, Eppie Lederer went beyond the call of duty, yet she made sure that she stayed in sync with her readers' views.

Meanwhile, Eppie's sister Popo was making headlines of her own. The Phillips family moved from the San Francisco area to Los Angeles in the spring of 1960. "Wherever my husband goes, I go," Popo announced at the time. She grew to love the glamorous lifestyle of Los Angeles, and she felt warmly welcomed in the city when an organization named Helping Hand named her "Mother of the Year" and honored her at a luncheon at the Beverly Hilton Hotel. After her second book, *Dear Teen-Ager*, was published that same year, Popo joked, "They call me the matron saint of teenagers."

Popo's professional advisors included recognized authorities in the fields of medicine and psychiatry, and her staff of eight helped with the constant onslaught of reader mail. She refused to hire a press agent or a manager, relying instead on her husband for business counseling. Popo's home life continued to be rewarding: her kids were contented, drug-free college students by this time, and her marriage to Mort Phillips remained strong.

In 1962 Popo (as Abigail Van Buren) launched a radio version of her column as a daily feature on CBS. The following year, Mort became president of the family corporation known as Ed Phillips and Sons, and he and Popo moved to Minnesota. Their daughter, Jeannie, who had graduated from UCLA, continued to script the *Dear Abby* radio show in her mother's absence.

In 1964 Popo flew to Sioux City to accept an honorary Doctorate of Humane Letters from her alma mater, Morningside College. Eppie too received the degree, but since the sisters were still feuding, they had requested separate ceremonies for the honors.

At the end of their first decade as advice columnists, both Eppie and Popo made significant changes in their careers. The *Sun-Times* syndicate finally presented Eppie with full ownership of the *Ann Landers* name, simultaneously publishing "A Love Letter to Ann Landers" in *Editor & Publisher* that declared, "We love Eppie so much [that] we all want to tell her we hope she'll stick around for at least 100 more years." Not to be outdone, Popo suddenly changed syndicates. Her new contract with the Tribune Company was heralded in a three-page color advertisement in the same trade journal in which Eppie's "love letter" appeared. The move not only increased Popo's profits, but it also scored a few dozen additional newspapers in which "Dear Abby" appeared. Soon Popo could boast a lead of 100 papers more than her sister.

No matter which of the two was "winning," it was clear that by the mid-1960s Ann Landers and Abigail Van Buren were the two top-ranked advice columnists in the United States, nearly eliminating all competitors. But for this reason, neither could afford to become irrelevant. The main challenge facing both Ann and Abby was keeping abreast of what was sometimes called the "new morality," becoming more progressive in their public views without completely forsaking their conventional values. Both sisters recognized the enormity of the task. "The world has gotten racier and I feel I must respond to what is going on out there. If I'm going to be useful, I'm going to have to deal with all kinds of human problems," Eppie commented. And her savvy sister had to agree.

Divorce survivor Ann Landers leaves her handprints in cement for a Chicago restaurant's "Sidewalk of the Stars" display. Shortly after her 36-year marriage to Jules Lederer ended, Ann wrote a heart-wrenching column to her readers: "Perhaps there is a lesson [here] for all of us," she said. "Never say, 'It couldn't happen to us!'"

7

WAKE UP AND SMELL THE COFFEE

In 1975, six years after Ann Landers published her heartfelt tribute to married life, she printed another personal column that contained a surprising revelation:

Dear Readers: In my 20 years as Ann Landers this is the most difficult column I have ever put together. . . .

The sad, incredible fact is that after 36 years of marriage Jules and I are being divorced. As I write these words, it is as if I am referring to a letter from a reader. It seems unreal that I am writing about my own marriage. . . .

That we are going our separate ways is one of life's strangest ironies. How did it happen that something so good for so long didn't last forever? The lady with all the answers doesn't know the answer to this one.

Perhaps there is a lesson there for all of us. At least, it is there for me. "Never say, 'It couldn't happen to us!'" . . .

Not only is this the most difficult column I ever have written, but also it is the shortest. I apologize to my editors for not giving you your money's worth today. I ask that you not fill this space with other letters. Please leave it blank—as a memorial to one of the world's

best marriages that didn't make it to the finish line.
                                            —Ann Landers

●   ●   ●

Dear Abby: What happened to you? You used to encourage married couples to do everything within their power to save their marriages. Lately, you give the impression that divorce could be the answer for some couples. Why?
                                         —Faithful Reader

Dear Reader: Because I think it's more important to save people than marriages. And in some cases, in an effort to save a marriage that isn't worth saving, people have destroyed themselves and each other.

●   ●   ●

For two decades Ann Landers, playing the role of the devoted wife in a happy, solid relationship, served as one of the country's most well-known advocates for making marriage work. But her own marriage was in fact difficult, with her husband being an admitted workaholic. As daughter Margo explained, "Father's interest in business was undiluted and wholehearted. When he wasn't actually working, he was talking about it, usually to Mother."

Jules was working 16 hours a day for Budget Rent-a-Car, a discount auto rental company he'd established in the late 1950s. In just a few years, Budget franchises had spread across the United States, eventually expanding into Europe, Mexico, and South Africa to become the third-largest car rental company in the world.

Eppie's husband was also an enthusiastic Scotch drinker and cigarette smoker, habits that his wife deplored—and harshly criticized in her columns. One of Jules's nicknames for his wife was "Carry Nation," the name of a famous female temperance leader who

crusaded against alcohol at the turn of the century.

Like her husband, Eppie Lederer was utterly devoted to her job. Despite her public stand that women should always put their marriages ahead of their careers, in reality Eppie spent far more time being Ann Landers than being Mrs. Jules Lederer. "I learned my work habits from Jules," Eppie often claimed. What she hid from public view was the fact that their "home life" consisted mainly of a husband and wife hard at work at two very separate desks.

By 1971 Jules had begun seeing another woman. He had recently sold the Budget Rent-a-Car company to Transamerica, and according to Eppie, "He had lost his identity. The principal support of his ego structure was shattered. The eternal optimist, the affable, hard-driving dynamo, began to come apart at the seams— and so did our marriage."

When a series of ill-fated investment deals resulted

Jeannie Phillips (right), shown here with her mother, Abigail Van Buren, and actress Meredith MacRae, served as scriptwriter for the Dear Abby *radio program.*

In 1973 Abby's daughter, Jeannie, married civil liberties lawyer Luke McKissack, whose clients had included Sirhan Sirhan, Robert F. Kennedy's assassin. "I hope this marriage takes," Abby quipped after helping plan the wedding, "because I can't go through this again."

in serious financial setbacks for Jules, Eppie assumed management of the household finances. She decided to purchase a new apartment for the family, and she spent huge sums decorating their new 15th-floor residence on Lake Shore Drive, installing wall panels imported from a British castle and artwork by Pablo Picasso and Pierre-Auguste Renoir. After all, Eppie Lederer was still Ann Landers, confident in herself and in her continuing success.

Jules, however, preferred their townhouse in London to the expansive Chicago residence, which he referred to as the "bowling alley." That he was living in

England with a 25-year-old nurse became public knowledge before long, but Eppie was one of the last to learn about her husband's "arrangement" abroad.

Like her mother, Margo Lederer did not complete her formal education, electing instead to drop out of Boston's Brandeis University and get married. John Coleman was a 26-year-old investment consultant from a well-to-do Jewish family, but Eppie did not approve of the marriage and attempted—unsuccessfully—to talk her daughter out of it.

By the late 1960s Margo had given her parents three young grandchildren, but she was also undergoing psychoanalysis. After she completed the therapy, she divorced John Coleman. "I stayed completely out of it," Eppie told a reporter at the time. "I had absolutely no advice to give." But her daughter's experience made a lasting impression on Ann Landers, who began to alter her rigid stance on saving one's marriage at any cost. After Margo's divorce, Ann Landers wrote, "I no longer believe that marriage means forever no matter how lousy it is—or [that couples should stay together] 'for the sake of the children.'"

In May 1970 Margo began writing her own column for the *Chicago Tribune*, a rival paper of her mother's employer. As the *Tribune*'s new "youth columnist," Margo wrote social commentary—and commuted to work from her 17-room apartment in a sleek Rolls Royce. Six months after the column debuted, it was picked up by Marshall Field, the same syndicate that handled the "Ann Landers" column. Margo interviewed numerous celebrities and even dated some of them, like Erich Segal, the author of the best-selling novel *Love Story*. In June 1972, however, she married a Jewish undertaker named Jules Furth. Ann Landers told her readers, "Apparently some people must live through one unsuccessful marriage to know how to make a second marriage work."

While the Lederer family was experiencing difficult

times, the Phillipses were going through their own changes. After attending Stanford University in Palo Alto, California, Eddie Phillips transferred to the University of Minnesota, earning a master's in clinical psychology and a law degree before joining the Phillips family business. In 1975, he took his father's place as president and CEO of Ed Phillips and Sons, which by that time was owned by Alco Standard. Four years earlier, Eddie had married Deanna (Dee-Dee) Pfafer, a divorced mother, and adopted her son. By 1972, the couple had produced a second grandson for Popo and Mort.

Jeannie had become deeply troubled, meanwhile, during her five-year stint as the scriptwriter for the *Dear Abby* radio program. With her mother's encouragement, Jeannie sought psychotherapy, and she eventually quit the show. "I wanted something that would permit me to be more expressive for myself," she explained.

In 1973, 30-year-old Jeannie married Luke McKissack, a civil liberties lawyer who had defended such infamous clients as the black radical Huey Newton and Sirhan Sirhan, Robert F. Kennedy's assassin. McKissack was not Jewish, but Popo approved of the marriage, declaring, "He's a beautiful man." Guests at the new couple's wedding reception, which was held at the Beverly Wilshire Hotel, ranged from black militants to the mayor of Beverly Hills. After coordinating two marriage ceremonies in two years, Popo joked, "I hope this marriage takes, because I can't go through this again."

Once Mort Phillips had turned over the helm of the family business to his son, he moved his wife back to the Los Angeles area. The couple purchased a sprawling brick house in the exclusive neighborhood called Bel-Air. There Popo installed her expansive collection of monkey artifacts and set up her typewriter in an office lined in yellow velvet. Although her radio show had been canceled the previous year after a successful 12-year run, Popo was overjoyed to return full-time to the Los Angeles office of "Dear Abby." Soon after,

Mort established Westland Capital Corporation, an investment company that provided advice to small businesses. A devoted family man, Mort said, "I'm teased a little bit for having a wife who's a successful working woman, and there are those who refer to me as Morton Van Buren, but it hasn't changed our way of living." Having weathered decades of moves and adjustments, Mort and Popo Phillips had managed to remain happily married.

Even after her divorce, Ann Landers continued her charitable work under the Lederer name. Here, she stands in front of a building named after her by the Menninger Foundation, a world-famous psychiatric center.

In September 1974 Popo's sister continued her habit of traveling abroad when as Ann Landers she traveled to China as part of an exchange visit sponsored by the American Medical Association. The only nonphysician in the group, Eppie toured hospitals and factories and sent back a week's worth of columns describing everyday Chinese life. Eppie learned a lesson, too, about "minding my own business, which seems to be an old Chinese custom."

At home in Chicago, meanwhile, many people were discussing Ann Landers's own private life. Jules had been introducing his girlfriend to the Lederers' friends, boldly squiring his live-in companion to restaurants and other public places. Finally, he confessed his love for the Englishwoman and admitted that he wanted a divorce—but he did not admit it to Eppie. Instead, he told Margo.

"He kept promising he would talk with Mother but somehow never did," Margo recounts in her biography of Eppie. Three months later, Margo gave her father an ultimatum. "I told him if he didn't tell Mother within one more month's time, I would." He didn't, so Margo tactfully advised her mother, "I think you should check on the state of your marriage." When Eppie confronted her husband the next day, Jules admitted his love affair and expressed interest in setting up what Eppie regarded as an out-of-the-question "arrangement."

In a 1995 interview with the *New Yorker*, Eppie recalled the painful confrontation. "I said, 'I'm glad you told me. The marriage is over.' 'Oh,' he said, quite surprised. 'Maybe we can work something out.' I said, 'No. No way.' He asked me to give him a few months to move out. I said, 'I'm not going to give you a lot of time, but I'll give you some time.' Finally, it occurred to me that he wasn't going to move out. He was just hanging around hoping I'd change my mind. Five weeks went by, and he [was] still there."

In the end, Eppie sent her husband of 36 years packing. "I said good-bye and good luck. And that was it," Eppie remembered. Margo concurs: "I don't think she had three bad days, total, after Father broke the news. She behaved as she would have told others to behave: 'Kwitcher bellyachin' buttercup,' is how she often put it in the column."

"It never occurred to me that I might fold up or break down or not be able to deal with it," Eppie explained. Instead, her major concern was that the divorce might put an end to her credibility as Ann Landers, advisor to the lovelorn, and thus ruin her career. "Some editors and readers could have said, 'Who is this woman to give advice when she can't even manage her own life?'" she told *People* magazine a few years later. "I feared that would be the judgment even though I didn't feel that way. I always thought I could manage my own life very well. The divorce was something beyond me. It wasn't anybody's fault."

After Eppie's husband moved out, reporters and camera crews camped out in the lobby of Eppie's apartment building looking for a statement from her, for sordid details of the break, or for candid photos of tears and trauma. To all uninvited inquiries about the details of her difficult divorce, Ann Landers simply responded with what amounted to an "M.Y.O.B.B."—which *Newsweek* defined as "a favorite Landerism for 'Mind your own business, Buster.'"

Eppie turned to her family for comfort and support, and she also flew to Notre Dame, Indiana, to talk with close friend Father Theodore Hesburgh. After a five-and-a-half-hour discussion with her confidant, Eppie Lederer was ready to move on. "I knew exactly where I was going," she said in 1980. "I'd always felt it was more important to be a wife than to be Ann Landers. But all of the energy I used to expend buying his socks and his shorts is now time and energy for myself."

After Eppie published her column about her intended divorce, she discovered to her surprise that her personal tragedy actually increased her credibility. Ann Landers had finally discovered what her readers had been trying to tell her for years: not all marriages work out, and that's okay. Her fans appreciated the fact that she was willing to admit in print that she had been wrong, and they loved her even more now that she seemed as vulnerable as many of them felt. She was buoyed by her readers' sympathetic response to her announcement, and she still keeps the 30,000 letters she received in response to that column in shoe boxes in her bedroom closet.

Eppie agreed to divorce in March 1975. Then she called her sister Popo, who flew to Chicago to be with her twin. Eppie stated afterward that her twin was "wonderful," but Popo thought that her sister really

At their 40th high school reunion in 1976, Abby (center) and Ann (right) share a moment with an acquaintance. Although the twin sisters have long since settled their highly publicized feud, they still disagree on exactly how they patched up their relationship.

didn't seem to need her support. "She had her head together," Popo summarized. "She didn't need anyone to help her."

Over the years there had been other reunions between the twins, and the sisters had eventually become friendly again. But the relationship was tenuous, and it took time for them to warm up to one another. At Margo's first wedding in 1961, it had been embarrassingly obvious that the twins were not on speaking terms. By the time of Eddie Phillips's marriage in 1971, however, the sisters were at least able to joke with one another about Eppie's dazzlingly inappropriate white mink—hardly a necessity at the late-summer reception.

Popo maintains that Eppie first broke the ice by telephoning her as early as 1964 to suggest a trip together to celebrate their mutual 25th wedding anniversary. Eppie remembers it differently. She claims that Abby telephoned *her* to ask, "'Can't we be friends again?' I felt it was time we were and said yes."

In 1976 the twins traveled to Sioux City together for their 40th high school reunion, where they appeared to enjoy one another's company as much as they delighted in the fawning attention of their former classmates. It was their first public appearance together in years. Yet, as late as 1981, the advice sisters were still squabbling in print. In a 1979 interview with *Ladies Home Journal*, Ann Landers called their rivalry "a problem" that she "soon forgot about," but Abby conducted a follow-up interview with the same popular women's magazine. Her words on the split with her sister were harsh and seemingly uncensored: "Those were very, very tough years," she complained. "Stony silence—stony, stony, stony," Popo said about what she saw as Eppie's unnecessary rejection of her. "She kept that chip on her shoulder for years. . . . I didn't set out to compete. I simply took the opportunity. She may think that if it were not for Dear Abby, she could have had the whole world!" But Popo appeared willing to risk more years of "stony, stony, stony" silence when she concluded, "I always got what Sis wanted. . . . If she looked old, if she needed a face lift, believe me, it's because she needed it. I'm quite opposed to chopping myself up, but it was her right. Why not? When you cry a lot, it's got to show."

According to Margo, "Mother's reaction was not to respond." But newspapers across the country picked up the story, quoting from the *Ladies Home Journal* articles and perpetuating the public perception of the twins as openly hostile advice sisters who not only did not speak to each other but also seemed incapable of speaking kindly about one another.

In 1976, one year after Eppie's divorce from Jules,

her daughter's marriage to Jules Furth also ended. Shortly after, Margo interviewed actor Ken Howard for her column. The two fell in love. Three months later, Margo married the blond heartthrob, cocreator and star of the popular TV series *The White Shadow*. According to Margo, her mother was "thrilled" over the marriage, even though Howard was of a different faith. As Ann Landers, Eppie soon made it a point to inform her readers that she had been wrong in her generalized disapproval of interfaith marriages.

Meanwhile, the real-life experiences of Popo Phillips forced her, as Abby, to update her views on marriage and divorce. In 1983, both of her children's relationships fell apart. Jeannie's childless marriage ended quietly, but Eddie's split with Dee-Dee made news when his wife contested the proposed divorce settlement. Dee-Dee's lawyer bragged to the press that she wanted $10 million, but she eventually settled for considerably less, an amount that the divorce judge termed "what the court would like to believe is a dose of reality."

Although Eppie and Popo's own relationship with one another remained troubled, they both continued to prove extremely adept at defeating adversity, constantly rethinking their personal views to keep up not only with the events in their private lives but also with the changes in society. "I'm always changing," Ann Landers declared. "Anyone who doesn't change their ideas over a period of years is either pickled in alcohol or embedded in wood."

Now in their eighties, neither Abigail Van Buren (left) nor Ann Landers is even considering retirement. "People usually retire to do what they really want to do," says Ann, "and I'm already doing that."

8

AMERICA'S
ADVICE SISTERS

By 1985 Ann Landers had written a total of 10,585 columns and selected 31,755 letters to answer in print. To every correspondent who had included an address, Ann Landers had sent a personal reply, bringing her total number of letters to more than 8.3 million. Around the same time, Eppie Lederer was happily dating. Typically Eppie's beaus were about 10 years younger than she—and they were always successful, professional men with plenty of energy. "I cannot imagine my life without a man," she told *Time* magazine in 1989. "I think when I'm 90 I'll still have a fella."

Eppie faced another significant life change in 1987, when she switched the "Ann Landers" column from the *Chicago Sun-Times* to its rival newspaper, the *Tribune*. The move freed Eppie from a restrictive contract so that she could forge a new deal in which she—like Popo had with "Dear Abby"—retained all rights to her own work.

As Ann Landers, Eppie had already authored a string of best-selling books under the rules of her old contract, including *Since You Ask Me* (1961), *Ann Landers Talks to Teenagers About Sex* (1963),

Ann Landers Says: Truth Is Stranger (1968), *The Ann Landers Encyclopedia* (1978), and *Ann Landers Speaks Out* (1978). With her new contract, Eppie Lederer would be free to publish books, pamphlets, and columns at her own discretion, knowing that not only the majority of her profits but also business choices would finally be her own.

By this time, "Ann Landers" was read by an estimated 85 million people and appeared in 1,100 newspapers around the world, so the *Sun-Times* was hard-hit by the loss of its popular columnist. The paper's desperate editors quickly announced a contest—similar to the one Eppie Lederer had entered some 32 years before—for the vacant advice columnist post. The contest attracted 12,000 applicants aged 4 to 85 and included convicts, actresses, lawyers, and housewives.

Two writers were eventually selected to fill Ann Landers's high heels: Jeffrey Zaslow was a 29-year-old reporter from the *Wall Street Journal* and was assigned to pen the offbeat "All That Zazz" column, while Diane Crowley, the 48-year-old daughter of Ruth Crowley, the original Ann Landers, wrote a more traditional column called "Dear Diane." Zaslow and Crowley moved into Ann Landers's cloyingly pink office at the *Sun-Times*, where they shared a single page in the paper five times a week.

A media blitz followed the selection of Zaslow and Crowley, both of whom appeared on *The Oprah Winfrey Show* and conducted countless other TV, radio, and print interviews.

Despite the media hype that accompanied the replacement duo, the new columnists soon admitted that they were "underwhelmed" with mail from readers. "I've gotten some nice letters," Zaslow reported. "And then someone sent back one of my columns with 'boaring, boaring, boaring [sic]' written across it. The other day I got another one that started off, 'Dear Zasshole.'"

By the mid-1980s, Abigail Van Buren had become

more selective about her public appearances, content to spend more of her time as Popo Phillips. But she dismissed rumors of retirement, joking that "Mother Confessors don't retire; they just turn up the volume on their hearing aids." Eppie agreed with her sister about the improbability of retirement. "I can't imagine why I would," she said. "People usually retire to do what they really want to do and I'm already doing that."

On the weekend of their 50th high school reunion, the Friedman twins addressed their former classmates in the ballroom of the Sioux City Hilton. Popo's speech drew laughs, but Eppie chose a more serious approach and presented her definition of success: "If you have a good name, if you are right more often than you are wrong, if your children respect you, if your grandchildren are glad to see you, if your friends can count on you and you can count on them in time of trouble, if you can face your God and say I have done my best,

With celebrity authors Tippi Hedren (far left), Sidney Sheldon (back row, left), John DeLorean (back row, right), and Janet Leigh (far right), best-selling author Abigail Van Buren attends a Beverly Hills bookstore event in 1985. The success of both Abby's and Ann Landers's books are proof that their advice still strikes a chord with readers.

then you are a success."

It was clear to the Central High Class of 1936 that the Friedman twins were now getting along nicely. Eppie had forgiven her sister for all of the attacks Popo had made in print, explaining, "The alternative is to write her off. I can't do it. It's too painful. . . . I refuse to allow myself to be miserable." At long last the advice sisters appeared ready, willing, and fully able to follow their own best counsel and once and for all "forgive and forget."

Since that time both sisters have avoided all but the most terse public discussion of their former feuding days. In *Wake Up and Smell the Coffee*, Ann Landers deflects the issue by saying, "I have been asked repeatedly if it is true that my twin (who writes as Dear Abby) and I do not speak. The answer is '*No*. It is not true.' We *do* speak—a lot. And often to each other."

Their personal rivalry now under control, the sisters have continued to speak out—candidly and often amid great controversy—on just about every other issue. In 1991, a letter advocating abortion rights was pulled from the "Dear Abby" column by the *New York Post*, whose editors substituted a less controversial letter about a teenager's dating concerns. Although the *Post* claimed that there was "not sufficient room" to print the exchange on abortion, New York's *Village Voice* claimed that the decision was politically motivated. An irate Abby demanded that the *Post* rerun the column at a later date. (It did.)

Both columnists have been the ideological targets of conservative organizations that take issue with their political views. But Ann and Abby do not allow their critics to intimidate them or to squelch their voices when discussing timely issues such as sex education in schools (they're both for it), access to birth control for teenagers (Ann and Abby believe it is important), and affirmative action for black job-seekers (they agree it's necessary). The advice sisters have also received plenty of flak over the years for their opinions on nuclear dis-

armament, gun control, and government funding of social programs. "Listen, if you stand for something, you cannot have everyone love you," says Popo. "If you don't take a stand on anything, you stand for nothing."

Eppie estimates that these days, one out of every 500 letters Ann Landers receives comes from someone seeking medical advice. Although she never provides direct answers to such questions, she does serve on the advisory boards of the American Cancer Society, the Mayo Foundation, Harvard and Yale Universities, and other powerful organizations. She turns to renowned experts from across the country for help in responding to letters on such issues as AIDS and the ethics of practicing euthanasia. And she continuously advises her readers to be more assertive when dealing with the medical establishment.

As Abby, Popo too has addressed a wide array of medical topics. She was an early advocate for the "Living Will," a legal document that reserves a patient's

Replacing a legend is never easy—just ask these two. After Ann Landers decided in 1987 to move her column from the Chicago Sun-Times *to its rival, the* Tribune, *the* Sun-Times *tried to replace her with Diane Crowley (left) and Jeffrey Zaslow. The two were received less than enthusiastically by the newspaper's readership.*

Still able to command the public's attention, Ann Landers receives a flu shot from Acting Surgeon General Audrey F. Manley in October 1996. Ann was invited to appear at this public health news conference to alert people about the dangers of the upcoming flu season.

right to turn down lifesaving technology in the event of a serious illness or accident. She has also taken on sensitive subjects such as nursing home abuse and inadequate funding for AIDS research.

Curiously, the sisters' columns on controversial political topics have not received as much public fanfare as their opinions on odd, seemingly trivial topics. When Ann Landers printed her favorite recipe for meat loaf, she received almost 100,000 letters from readers who found it inedible and felt compelled to tell her so. When she wrote a column describing the proper way to hang toilet paper—positioned so that the tissue falls along the wall, rather than over the top of the roll— some 15,000 readers cared enough to forward their own opinions on the matter.

When Abby responded to a correspondent who wondered whether Native American men ever lost their hair, she asked her readers to send in photos proving that it was true. She was besieged with mail—and photos. And she still remembers the strangest letter she ever received: "I got a letter once from a man who was in love with his pony. I mean really in love—we got a picture of the pony, so help me. If I had printed it, people would think I was making it up." But she has no reason to make up anything, she says. "There's nothing weirder than what I get in the mail."

Lately, Eppie's twin has taken to warning readers of her "Ann Landers" column about the dangers of online romances after she received a letter from a woman who had been raped and nearly killed by a man she met on the Internet. Although she praises computers as an educational tool, Eppie still relies on her trusty IBM electric typewriter—and she hoards typewriter ribbons in a closet in case they become obsolete some day. "That machine has to last as long as I do," she told the *New York Times* a few years ago.

At 80, Eppie Lederer fully intends to make that old machine last. She still reviews her letters in the privacy of her lavish Chicago apartment. Sometimes she pores over her letters in the evening while relaxing in the bathtub, or she reads them while sitting in bed at the end of the day. Sometimes, she is still typing at 2:00 A.M.

Every day, about 2,000 letters arrive at Ann Landers's *Chicago Tribune* office, where her staff carefully whittles down the pile to the 500 Eppie will examine at home. She always chooses the ones she will answer and then writes the column herself. "Only I can write the column," Eppie states. "I extract the guts of the letter. I make sure it is grammatical. I edit. I do as little editing as possible. [But] you wouldn't believe the profanity," she says.

People tell great-grandmother Eppie Lederer that she looks more like 50 than her real age. She eats whatever she wants, but has not touched a steak in 25 years. "I seem to like the foods that are good for me," Eppie claims, although she admits to having a passion for chocolate—*good* chocolate. She exercises daily by practicing yoga and doing stretches, which are followed by brisk walks around her spacious apartment. "It's an obstacle course," she jokes. "Don't hit the Picasso and don't bump the bust by Dali." When weather permits, Eppie walks the 16 blocks to her newspaper office, as her chauffeur-driven limousine follows behind her at a respectful distance.

Sister Popo's passion for Godiva chocolates does not show on her slim, youthful figure. "I used to exercise by standing in front of an open window and winding my watch," Popo teases. She still lives and works in fine style in her home office in Beverly Hills, where daughter Jeannie now serves as her mother's editor. "People are shocked by some of the things I discuss in my column," Abby informed *People* magazine in 1998, "but that's their ignorance. You can't help that."

"I'm really quite an ordinary person, you know, who's had extraordinary good luck," Popo Phillips confides. "Right time. Right place. That's a cliché, but I don't have any illusions about myself. I've led a charmed life, I'm so happy and I haven't missed a thing. Plee-e-ease, if I go tomorrow," she declares, "nobody cry for me." Eppie Lederer also believes she has been extraordinarily fortunate in life. "I think there's such a thing as serendipity," she says. "You have to be lucky. You have to be at the right place at the right time. But once you are lucky, you have to know what to do with your luck."

If either of these two energetic and opinionated octogenarians, the ever-popular and extra-lucky Friedman twins, were to "go tomorrow," they would certainly be missed—by "Scared" and "Finished at Twenty-Four," "Hoping" and "Not Dumb," "Wondering" and "Resident of the World's Largest Open-Air Lunatic Asylum,"

DEAR ABBY,
Happy Birthday
to
America's Favorite
Columnist
Love ♥
90 Million Fans
HERSHEY'S COCOA

A notorious chocolate-lover, Abigail Van Buren receives a tasty birthday gift from the Hershey Chocolate Company. Abby's love of sweets does not show in her slim figure, although she claims that she used to exercise "by standing in front of an open window and winding my watch."

not to mention the millions of other "Faithful Readers" around the globe. For more than 40 years, Ann Landers and Abigail Van Buren have brought their own special brand of wit and wisdom—including not only puns and political hot potatoes but also unabashed caring and sound advice—into our living rooms, kitchens, commuter trains, and offices. In spite of their own personal problems, or perhaps because of them, the world's two "best listeners" continue to offer intimate expressions of concern to an increasingly alienated society. Ann and Abby are still there for us. And they will undoubtedly *both* have the last word.

CHRONOLOGY

1918   Esther Pauline ("Eppie") and Pauline Esther ("Popo") born on July 4 in Sioux City, Iowa, to Abraham and Rebecca Friedman

1936   Eppie and Popo graduate from Central High School and enroll in Sioux City's Morningside College

1939   The twins marry in a double wedding ceremony on July 2, Eppie to Jules Lederer and Popo to Morton Phillips

1940   Margo Lederer born in Sioux City

1942   Jeannie Phillips born in Minneapolis, Minnesota

1945   Edward Phillips born in Minneapolis; the Phillips family moves to Eau Claire, Wisconsin; the Lederer family follows within weeks

1954   Eppie is elected county chair for the Democratic Party of Eau Claire; she resigns when the Lederers move to Chicago, Illinois

1955   The Phillips family moves to the San Francisco area; Eppie is selected as the new Ann Landers by the *Chicago Sun-Times*

1956   Popo convinces the *San Francisco Chronicle* to hire her to write "Dear Abby"

1957   *Dear Abby*, Popo's first book, is published by her syndicate

1959   Jules Lederer founds Budget Rent-a-Car; Ann Landers visits the Soviet Union

1961   *Since You Ask Me*, Ann Landers's first book, is published

1963   A radio version of the "Dear Abby" column begins its 12-year run on CBS radio

1967   Ann Landers visits U.S. troops in Vietnam

1971   Ann Landers is awarded American Cancer Society's National Service award

1974   Ann Landers visits China; Abby Van Buren receives the Margaret Sanger Award from National Planned Parenthood

1975   Ann Landers and Jules Lederer divorce

1979   Abby Van Buren is awarded an honorary chair at the first National Women's Conference on Cancer; Ann Landers receives the Margaret Sanger Award

1987   Eppie moves her Ann Landers column from the *Chicago Sun-Times* to the *Chicago Tribune*

1998   Eppie and Popo celebrate their 80th birthday

BIBLIOGRAPHY

Buckley, Christopher. "You Got a Problem?" *New Yorker*, 4 December 1995.

Grossvogel, David I. *Dear Ann Landers: Our Intimate and Changing Dialogue with America's Best-Loved Confidante.* New York: Contemporary Books, 1987.

Howard, Margo. *Eppie: The Story of Ann Landers.* New York: G.P. Putnam's Sons, 1982.

Landers, Ann. *The Best of Ann Landers.* Second edition. New York: Fawcett, 1997.

_____. *Wake Up and Smell the Coffee: Advice, Wisdom, and Uncommon Good Sense.* New York: Villard, 1996.

Morton, Danelle. "Answering Machine," *People Weekly*, 13 July 1998.

Pottker, Jan, and Bob Speziale. *Dear Ann, Dear Abby: The Unauthorized Biography of Ann Landers and Abigail Van Buren.* New York: Dodd, Mead & Company, 1987.

Van Buren, Abigail. *The Best of Dear Abby.* Second edition. New York: Andrews and McMeel, 1989.

_____. *Where Were You When President Kennedy Was Shot? Memories and Tributes to a Slain President as Told to Dear Abby.* New York: Andrews and McMeel, 1993.

INDEX

PICTURE CREDITS

Virginia Aronson is the author of more than 17 books, including textbooks on health, self-help guides, and biographies for young readers. She has written several titles for Chelsea House, most recently *How to Say No* in the JUNIOR DRUG AWARENESS series and *Women in Literature* in the FEMALE FIRSTS IN THEIR FIELDS series. Aronson lives in South Florida with her writer husband and their young son.

Matina S. Horner was president of Radcliffe College and associate professor of psychology and social relations at Harvard University. She is best known for her studies of women's motivation, achievement, and personality development. Dr. Horner has served on several national boards and advisory councils, including those of the National Science Foundation, Time Inc., and the Women's Research and Education Institute. She earned her B.A. from Bryn Mawr College and her Ph.D. from the University of Michigan, and holds honorary degrees from many colleges and universities, including Mount Holyoke, Smith, Tufts, and the University of Pennsylvania.